FURNITURE-MAKING PROJECTS FOR THE WOOD CRAFTSMAN

GUILD OF MASTER CRAFTSMAN PUBLICATIONS LTD

This collection first published 1999 by
Guild of Master Craftsman Publications Ltd,
Castle Place 166 High Street, Lewes,
East Sussex BN7 IXU

© GMC Publications 1999
ISBN I 86108 140 5

Reprinted 1999, 2000, 2001

A catalogue record of this book is available from the British library

Front cover photographs, left to right, top to bottom:
Paul Richardson, Michael Manni (2)
Chris Challis, Stephen Hepworth (2)

Back cover photographs:
Stephen Hepworth (top), Chris Skarbon (bottom)

Article photography by:
Anthony Bailey (pp. 30-1, 33, 38-41, 77-80), Chris Challis (89-90),
Stephen Hepworth (pp 14-18, 42-4, 55, 59, 72-3, 76, 84-6, 92-9, 108, 113),
Michael Manni (pp. 35, 37-40), John Morley (pp. 103-6), Tim Roberts (pp. 19-29).
Chris Skarbon (pp. 47-9, 51, 53-4), Studio Twelve Photography (pp. 66-70)

Other photographs by the authors.

Illustrations by Simon Rodway and Ian Hall unless otherwise stated.

Designed by Edward Le Froy and Jenni Keeble

Printed and bound by Kyodo Printing (Singapore) under the supervision of
MRM Graphics, Winslow, Buckinghamshire, UK

CONTENTS

NOTE

Every effort has been made to ensure that the information in this book is accurate at the time of writing but inevitably prices, specifications, and availability of tools will change from time to time. Readers are therefore urged to contact manufacturers or suppliers for up-to-date information before ordering tools.

MEASUREMENTS

Throughout the book instances may be found where a metric measurement has fractionally varying imperial equivalents, usually within ⅟₁₆in either way. This is because in each particular case the closest imperial equivalent has been given.

A mixture of metric and imperial measurements should NEVER be used – always use either one or the other.

See also detailed metric/imperial conversion charts on page 117.

INTRODUCTION

THERE IS EVERY CHANCE that the end of the 20th century will be looked back on as a golden age of furniture-making. At this time, makers are working in the widest range of idioms imaginable, as they have so much to choose from: the ages of oak and walnut precede the extraordinary 75 years or so that comprise what we call the Georgian period; the latter followed by the exuberant Regency style; Arts & Crafts from Morris to Mackintosh, Shaker from the USA; and of course the 20th Century itself – a rich palette by any standards.

As today's craftsmen can draw on such a continuing tradition, their work develops free of constraint on design. Likewise the diversity of techniques available to the furniture-maker has never been greater, traditional approaches such as dovetailing and morticing co-existing with biscuit joints, routed joints and high-tech adhesives.

Much of this development is driven by technology, not least in the new materials now offered – what would a Georgian craftsman make of MDF, for example?

It is in the small workshop that the blending of these elements is most noticeable. *Furniture & Cabinetmaking* magazine, from which this book is compiled, is unique in drawing out the experience of individual makers regardless of their style or approach, and presenting examples of their work in the form of projects. The result is a fascinating insight into the craft at its current stage of development, and an invaluable guide for practitioners.

Whatever your taste in furniture design and preference in techniques, the projects in this book will not only provide a useful source of ideas for furniture, but also some refreshing and innovative approaches to making it.

Paul Richardson
Managing Editor (Magazines)

A modified mule

In the first of two parts, Editor **Paul Richardson** starts work on an updated version of a classic piece of storage furniture

MAIN ILLUSTRATION BY IAN HALL

BELOW: Mule chest, modified to give doors rather than a lift-up lid

SOME PIECES of furniture stick in my mind, lodging firmly in the "I must get round to making one of those" section of my mental to-do list – which gets longer every day. One such piece is the relatively humble mule chest.

A mule chest is a sophistication of one of furniture's most basic forms; the storage box. The earliest chests, or coffers, were formed by joining six planks – front, back, sides, bottom and top – and though the planks later became panelled frames, the basic lidded box remained the fundamental storage solution for hundreds of years.

Ultimately the successor to the box-chest is the chest of drawers, but along the way came the rather nicely balanced mule chest – a box chest sitting on top of a couple of drawers.

Leaving aside the practicality of the piece, I find the visual balance of framed and fielded panels, above drawers with plate handles, especially pleasing. Add another of my favourites, bracket feet, and some nicely-figured quarter sawn oak, and a truly classic piece of English furniture results.

> "A mule chest is a sophistication of one of furniture's most basic forms; the storage box"

Modifications

I've been waiting for an opportunity to make one of these for years, and then two of my regular clients, Chris and Mel, made the mistake of telling me that they wanted a sideboard, but had no idea what kind.

hest

"You want something like a mule chest" I said.

The only drawback of the mule chest is the lift-up lid, making it unsuitable for display objects on top and requiring more leaning over to access the contents than most people want to be involved with. The panelled front, however, may be subverted into doors without visual clashing, and this allows the top to be fixed.

I drew two versions of this piece for the clients to choose from, one with square-panelled doors and another featuring the broken-arch panels shown here. With a little nudging, they chose the right one!

Selection

Unless you are very familiar with this kind of work, make up a full-size drawing on MDF, or similar, before starting. It is easier to work out the relationship of the parts with a pencil in your hand than with a saw.

With traditional oak furniture, the quality of the timber used is of paramount importance. The heavy

ABOVE: Shelf is adjustable, finely calculated to accommodate bottles below and glasses above

"It is easier to work out the relationship of the parts with a pencil in your hand than with a saw"

visual blocks involved must be broken up by colour, grain and texture to avoid a sombre, funereal look.

In this I was the beneficiary of a happy accident – the timber supplier failed to deliver when

arranged, and by way of apology supplied me with their very best selected quartered oak – I bought about 8 cu ft of generous 25mm (1in) thick stuff for this chest, which allowed for further selection as I made up the cutting list.

LEFT: Carcass sub-assemblies: side panel is tongue and grooved with a loose-fitted fielded panel; frame is mortice and tenoned – note notch for side facings

RIGHT: Side panel
biscuited ready
for assembly –
position mid-
panel biscuits
using drawer
divider as guide

There is only one way to get a cutting list out of waney-edged English oak while obtaining the best visual effect for critical components – and that is to lay out the boards on the workshop floor and mark out the parts with wax crayon, nesting them together to avoid wastage.

At least that's how I used to do it when I had a workshop floor to speak of. Now things are more cramped I have to stand all the boards on their long edges, flipping through them like a card index. It is worth spending time on this stage, though, to avoid the best figure ending up on internal parts!

Construction

Although this is a classic piece, I departed from traditional construction quite severely in places. The carcass sides and doors have, in place of mortice and tenons, tongue and groove joints. This is quite safe in this instance, as the solid panels add strength, and the stiles and rails are very wide, allowing a long joint. Glue technology is so much more advanced now than in the 18th century that, provided that the gluing area is large, mechanical strength is less important than it once was. Polyurethane glue, such as Gorilla Glue or Titebond Polyurethane, was used throughout and is a good

performer, which doesn't leave black stains on oak.

The panelled sides are held apart by jointed frames – morticed and tenoned this time – top and bottom, with a solid horizontal division between the drawers and the cupboard. These three horizontal carcass members are biscuit-jointed to the sides, and cut round the vertical facings which are also biscuited to the carcass sides.

A drawer divider is biscuited in place between bottom frame and fixed shelf.

The back is another mortice and tenoned frame, this time grooved to take loose panels – it extends down only to the fixed shelf, leaving the back of the drawer apertures open.

The drawers themselves are as conventional as they come, hand dovetailed and so on, and the bracket feet are made according to 18th century norms, complete with glue blocks. To allow the feet to sit wider than the carcass, a moulding is planted around the bottom of the carcass.

The top is slot-screwed to the top frame from below.

Sides and doors

Cut all parts from the sawn boards, then plane and thickness to finished sections.

I like to achieve a set of sub-assemblies as soon as possible, so the first job is to join the boards needed to make up wide components, in this case the panels, shelves and top. I biscuit these, but make sure that the biscuits are far enough away from the ends not to be revealed when cutting the panel-raise.

Now the frames for the sides and doors can be made up. Remember to add an allowance to the width of each door's inner stile for the closing rebates.

I used a pair of tongue and groove router cutters made by The Wealden Tool Co. for the jointing – they cut a 12mm (½in) long by 6mm (¼in) thick tongue on the ends of the rails, and a corresponding groove in the inner edge of the stiles and rails, which takes both the rails' tongues and the dry-fitted panels.

Don't even think of using a hand-held router for this job – a nice flat router table with a mitre guide is essential. Cut the tongues first, then the grooves. Leave the upper door rails square for this operation, cutting their arches, *see panel*, last of all before completing the groove – carefully! Before changing the cutter, groove a 150mm (6in) long piece of scrap.

"Don't even think of using a hand-held router for this job – a nice flat router table with a mitre guide is essential"

Panels

Now for the panel raising. This is another job for the router table, this time with a large diameter panel-raising cutter – this must have a guide bearing for the shaped work, although the straight edges are best fielded against a fence. These cutters are not safe at high speeds; only use them in variable speed routers, set to the slowest speed.

The aim is to produce a raising with a flat tongue which fits the groove in the stiles and rails; do this by gradually increasing the height of the cutter, checking for fit with the grooved piece of scrap – try this all the way round each panel, as the cut can vary. I find that two passes at each depth setting evens it out.

Make each pass across the ends of the panels first, then along the long grain, to avoid tearout.

That's all very well for the square side panels, but the broken arches of the door panels need a bit more work. Leave the panel square, but cut to width, while you field the bottom and sides of these – then complete the broken arch, *see panel*.

Finish-sand the panels, then glue-up the doors and side panels. If the rails' ends were square before assembly, it is hard to end up with an out-of-square panel, but I make these assemblies a little over-size to allow for final dimensioning after they are made up.

The side panels may now be rebated for the back, and the skirting board relief – if required – cut.

ABOVE: Finished in the white, and fitted up with hardware, ready for finishing

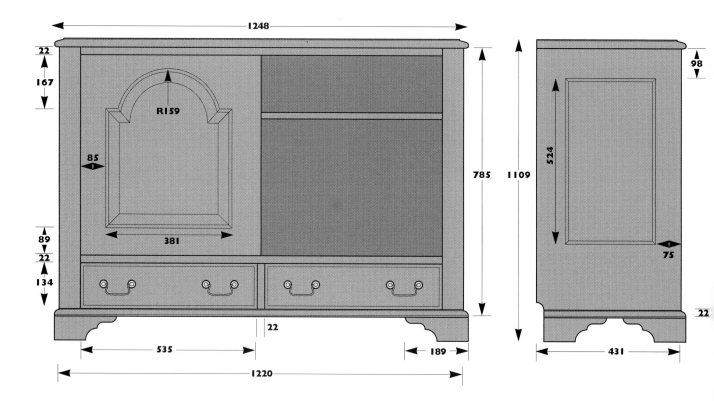

"If the rails' ends were square before assembly, it is hard to end up with an out-of-square panel"

Frames

Having used a tongue and groove joint for doors and sides, you might expect me to use them for the frames which make up the top, bottom and back of the carcass.

Wrong! The sections of the components involved, in relation to the overall size of the frames, are smaller, making for less gluing area and greater racking stresses. As a consequence, good old-fashioned mortice and tenons are used, which should please the purists. The inner edges of the back panel's frame are grooved for dry-fitted panels.

Again, I make these a little oversize and trim after assembly – note that the back panel is fixed straight onto the top frame and solid horizontal member, while it is rebated into the sides.

Top and bottom frames, and the solid carcass member which forms the floor of the cupboard, project in front of the carcass sides by the thickness of the side facings, *see main illustration*, and must be notched to accommodate them. I cut

these notches before assembly, but if you are feeling your way through this piece it might be better to glue-up first and then cut to fit.

Gluing-up

Before gluing-up, though, one more part must be made up – the drawer divider. This is made from two pieces of oak; the main part with grain running front-to-back, with a smaller piece to form a muntin rail biscuited to the front. This is, in turn, biscuited between the bottom frame and solid member.

All three horizontal parts should now be ready for biscuiting to the sides. Top and bottom are straightforward corner joints cut from the biscuit jointer's fence, the mid-panel joint for the solid member is made using the drawer divider as a guide for the jointer's base plate.

Having cut these, glue and cramp in the following order: first, make up the drawer divider, bottom frame and solid member as a sub-assembly, cramp and allow to dry;

next glue and cramp this and the top frame between the sides, paying particular attention to square and the lining up of front edges.

Once this lot is dry and cleaned up, cut notches for the side facings if you haven't already done so, then biscuit the facings to the edges of the sides. If you have a biscuit cutter for the router, it is possible to fit a biscuit across the top and bottom of these, inside the notches.

Clean up

Give everything a good clean up, planing the various bits that make up the front of the carcass flush, and rout a small V-groove along the join between sides and facings to tidy it up.

The main structure is now complete, which seems like a good time to pause. In the next article we do the twiddly bits. ▣

Full measured drawings for this piece are available free of charge. See next article for details.

"Good old-fashioned mortice and tenons are used, which should please the purists"

BROKEN ARCHES

Broken-arch panelled doors are a nice feature, but the working out can be tricky.

The flat inner area of the fielded panel must be topped with a full half-circle – this means that the outer perimeter of the panel is less than a full half-circle, as is the radiused inner edge of the top rail. Because the panel is grooved into the rail, its outer radius is greater than the rail's – I strongly recommend making a full-size drawing first!

Working from your drawing, mark out and cut the shape of the top rails first, finding the centre of the radius as described below.

Marking out

Working on the back of the panel, draw a centre line, top to bottom. Dry-assemble a door frame, then measure from the inner edge of the bottom rail to the inner edge of the shoulder of the arched top rail. Add twice the length of the tongue to this measurement to give the distance from the bottom of the panel to the cut line of the shoulder – mark this dimension (A) across the full width of the panel.

Next, starting from the point where this line crosses the centre line drawn earlier, measure back towards the bottom, a distance equal to the length of the tongue plus the width of the fielding (B). This gives you the centre of the various radii involved.

Now, starting again from the intersection of the shoulder cut line and the centre line, measure towards the top a distance equal to the height of the arch of the top rail (C), and mark.

With its point in the radius's centre mark, set a trammel to the arch top mark, and draw the radius.

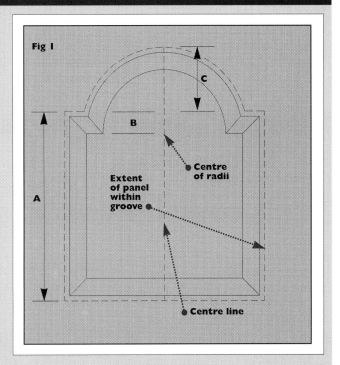

Fig I

C

B

● Centre of radii

Extent of panel within groove ●

A

● Centre line

Cutting

Cut the square shoulders, then the radius – this latter is best done with a router guided by a trammel. Clean up the internal corner with a chisel.

Now the fielding can be routed, on the router table as with the straight edges but this time using the cutter's guide

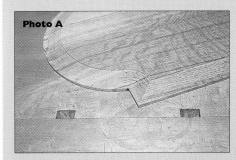

Photo A

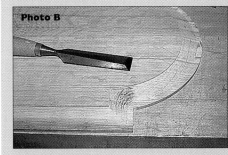

Photo B

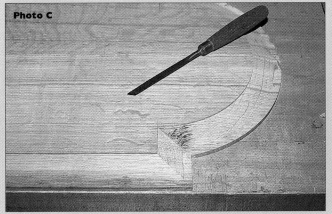

Photo C

bearing. Make no mistake about it, this is a bit scary, so use a start pin, ensure safe guarding – if necessary make a perspex guard fixed to the table and covering the cutter – and use temporary handles pinned to the back of each panel to feed the work. Go carefully, in shallow passes, until the correct depth is reached.

Chisel work

You will notice that the cutter leaves a radiused internal corner where the internal mitre should be, see photo A – this can only be completed by the use of chisels.

First define the quirk of the raised, flat part of the panel by scribing downwards with a wide chisel and paring a flat at the top of the chamfer, then doing the same for the tongue at the base of the chamfer, see photo B.

To be absolutely correct, the intersection of a curved moulding with a straight one should be a curve, but life's too short for that, frankly, so scribe a straight mitre line, again with a wide chisel, from corner to corner. Don't go too deep.

Now pare the chamfer of the shoulder, working in towards the mitre. A wide chisel will do most of this, but a skewed chisel will help to finish off. Complete this side of the mitre before proceeding, see photo C.

Finish the job by paring the arch's chamfer, again working towards the mitre, although you may find it easier to make the cuts across the grain.

This process sounds worse than it is – my carving skills are pretty feeble, but I managed to produce the results shown here quite quickly, see photo D.

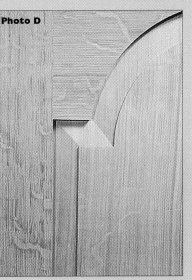

Photo D

A modified mule chest – part two

Editor **Paul Richardson** completes this traditional piece

IN THE FIRST PART of this project, *see page 2*, the main carcass was completed, and the arched-panel doors were prepared. This leaves what I call the fiddly bits.

Base moulding

First of the fiddly bits, starting at the bottom, are the bracket feet. The bracket foot is one of my favourite period details – as it is fitted slightly proud of the carcass it gives the piece an appearance of sitting firm and square on the floor, without looking as heavy as a solid plinth.

The other nice thing about bracket feet is that they are made from one-inch timber, so if using them, a whole piece can be made from one bought thickness.

Before the feet can be attached, though, a moulding must be added to the base of the carcass to provide

both a visual break and an extended ledge for the feet.

The moulding itself is a cove and bead – called a 'classical mould' by router cutter suppliers, though I wish they wouldn't. It is mitred at the corners, and while you are welcome to pin, biscuit or otherwise fix it on, the gluing area is so large that I simply glue and clamp it. The moulding must be flush with the bottom of the carcass.

Bracket feet

Each front foot comprises two shaped parts, mitred together – it is best to cut the mitres before the profile. The two parts are glued together and to the base of the carcass, then glue blocks are added inside the foot and to the carcass. Traditionally, Scotch glue was used for this due to its fast grab, meaning

ABOVE AND BELOW: **Mule chest as started last month**

that clamps were not needed, and I still use it unless the glue pot is cold, in which case I use a fast-setting PVA such as Franklins' Wood Moulding Glue. With either adhesive the parts are rubbed into position, held briefly while the glue grabs, then left to dry.

Pin the joint if you feel moved to do so; any slight openness of the mitre can be dealt with by lightly hammering the oak along the join.

The back feet are even easier – one shaped piece, one plain piece butted to it, and glue blocks along the inside of the joins.

> "The back feet are even easier – one shaped piece, one plain piece butted to it, and glue blocks along the inside of the joins"

Drawers

Next fiddly bits are the drawers. The openings are almost ready for them, but require kickers to be fitted to the outer runners. These are prepared to slightly less than the width of the internal measurement of the side facings, and glued in position.

The drawers themselves are the usual dovetailed affairs; you should have saved some highly figured oak for the fronts, and plain but quartered stuff for the sides and back.

With a chest of this kind thin, fine drawer sides look wrong and are not called for, so they are finished thick enough to be grooved for the bottoms.

Cut the fronts just too wide – by a millimetre, or a full thirty-second of an inch – to fit in the openings, then mark out and cut the sides' dovetails on the bandsaw. These are then transferred to the fronts and backs with a marking knife.

Cut the sockets for the tails fractionally deeper than the sides' thickness – more so in the backs – then glue-up, hammering the pins over to pinch the dovetails closed.

After cleaning up the sides, the drawers should be a near-fit. Adjust as necessary, then fit the bottoms, which slide into their grooves from the back and are screwed, through a slot, up into the drawer back.

Drawer stops can now be fitted; allow the drawers to sit inside the carcass front a little, as this will accentuate their edges – we aren't making a smooth, modern piece here, remember, so every element should be clearly defined.

POLISHING

When all the hardware is fitted satisfactorily, off it comes so that the chest can be polished.

The colour of this chest was to match other oak pieces in the clients' house, although it was not to be distressed, thankfully. I'd like to tell you how it was done, but can't, as due to time pressures the polishing was carried out by a friend of Technical Editor Alan Goodsell, called Ben, and he won't tell me!

"When all the hardware is fitted satisfactorily, off it comes so that the chest can be polished"

I can understand his reticence, in a way, as he specialises in period-style oak furniture that is distressed and, frankly, would fool me – it looks totally convincing.

I can tell you that the colour comes mostly from Van Dyke crystals, and the actual finish is a top secret beeswax recipe of Ben's own, as is the detail of the rest of the process.

I did, however, polish two chairs which I made for the same room, and achieved a similar appearance with Bollom's English Brown Oak grain filler, followed by a grubby French polish made by adding various spirit stains to garnet. This was cut back with 0000 wire wool and finished with button polish, then Liberon Black Bison wax.

ABOVE: Drawer apperture prepared with kicker and stop

Shelf

The chest's shelf is made from solid timber and, being adjustable, is not held flat by the structure. This means that it must be constructed in such a way as to allow for dimensional change due to changes in humidity, and the simplest method is to fit breadboard ends, or cleats.

To avoid the ends of the cleats being seen when the doors are opened, they are made slightly narrower than the internal depth of the side facings.

Make up the main part of the shelf by biscuiting together boards to achieve the depth required. When these are dry, square off the ends and rout a tongue on each, then rout a corresponding groove in one edge of each cleat – I used the same matched tongue-and-groove cutter set, from the Wealden Tool Company, for this as I

"With a chest of this kind thin, fine drawer sides look wrong and are not called for, so they are finished thick enough to be grooved for the bottoms"

used to make the door and side panel joints.

Glue and cramp the cleats, then trim when dry.

The shelf is supported by small brass pegs – these fit tightly into 5mm (³⁄₁₆in) holes drilled in the carcass sides, *see photo*, which is where the adjustability comes in. It is worth making a simple jig to drill the series of holes required – jig is a strong word, actually, since all it consists of is a strip of 6mm (¼in) MDF in which as many holes are drilled as desired – three, in my case. Place this jig in each corner of the carcass and drill through the holes – wear of the jig's holes isn't a problem, as each one is used only four times and the jig is disposable.

The shelf can sit directly onto these pegs, but it is neater if a small recess is routed for each support, *see photo,* and it is a good habit to get into.

Top

Like all of the wide components, the top is made up of narrower boards biscuit-jointed together. The top is critical in terms of appearance, though, so use two boards if possible and certainly no more than three.

It would look quite wrong to use cleats on the top, and even though it is slot-screwed to the carcass any deflection from flat will stick out like a sore thumb, so choose the most quarter-sawn boards you have – being oak, they will be the best looking boards anyway, so it's no great hardship.

Position the biscuits carefully, to avoid them being revealed when the

top is trimmed to size, and take special care when clamping that the top is flat – using sash cramps on alternate faces will help.

Trim the top to size when the glue is dry (why do we always say that in these projects – who's going to trim something while the glue is still wet?).

Rout the moulding round the front and side edges of the top – note that it is a cove and bead, as with the base moulding. With furniture of this period – by which I mean any time before the 20th century – keep the variety of mouldings to a bare minimum; the quickest way to turn a timeless classic into a tacky repro is to cover it with fiddly mouldings.

As mentioned above, the top is slot-screwed to the carcass. In fact, those screws through the front rail into the top are not fitted through slotted holes – they are plain, so that any shrinkage that occurs will not reduce the overhang at the front. The screws at the middle and back are fitted through slots, allowing movement at the back only.

Doors

Although the doors were made in part one of this project, there is still quite a lot of work to do on them. First they have to fit the opening, with the regulation not-very-big gap around them. They are also rebated together at the inner edge, and this should be done first.

The inner stiles should be 10mm (³⁄₈in) wider than the outer stiles, and each door should be 5mm (³⁄₁₆in) wider than half the width of the door opening: this is because the centre of

"With furniture of this period – by which I mean any time before the 20th century – keep the variety of mouldings to a bare minimum"

LEFT: Fit doors with carcass on a flat, level surface to avoid distortion

Full dimensioned drawings for this project are available free of charge to readers of F&C. Send a self-addressed A4 envelope bearing stamps to the value of 60p to: Mule Chest Drawings, Furniture & Cabinetmaking, GMC Publications Ltd, 86 High Street, Lewes, East Sussex, BN7 1XN.

ABOVE: **Bead to front of closing rebate, note door-stop and bolt slot**

ABOVE RIGHT: **Till lock and key provide catch and handle**

BELOW: **Top moulding is cove and bead to match base moulding**

the pair of doors, when they are closed together, passes though the middle of the rebates, giving 5mm (³⁄₁₆in) extra door width each side.

So that the doors look balanced, the door which is rebated on its inner face has a bead on its outer face of the same width as the rebate – 10mm (³⁄₈in) – so that the centre of the pair passes through the middle of the bead. If that doesn't make sense – I accept this is a possibility! – draw it out full-size, and you'll see what I mean.

Once the closing rebates and bead have been done, the doors should be fitted to the opening as a pair. I place veneer shims all round, and when the doors sit firmly in the opening with the shims in place, it's a fit.

While fitting the doors, by the way, make sure that the carcass is sitting on a flat, level surface so that it doesn't distort. If the floor isn't level at the chest's eventual destination the feet can be shimmed until the carcass is square – fit the doors to an out of square carcass, though, and when siting the piece to make the doors work you'll be shimming to force the carcass into wind, which is pretty insane.

I use my bench as a register surface as it is level, flat and big enough – and as a bonus find fitting-up much easier at this working height.

As I said in part one of this project, I have wanted to make this piece for years, and I was pleased with the result. Not a ground-breaking piece of furniture design, but a useful development of a classic form and one which will find favour with many people.

That'll do me. ∎

HARDWARE

After fitting the brass butt hinges to the doors, it is logical to fit the other hardware. Always fit up before the piece is polished, ignoring the temptation to leave it till later.

I've never seen a door handle that looks right on this kind of furniture. The plate handles fitted to the drawers have a matching drop handle, but they look too fiddly altogether. Effective catches for a meeting pair of doors are thin on the ground, too, but luckily both problems can be solved at a stroke by using a till lock and flush bolts. This allows for a modest wire escutcheon to be fitted, and the key, left in the lock, functions as an effective handle.

The flush bolts used here are, although nicely made themselves, supplied with a nasty bit of bent sheet brass intended as a door stop and catching plate for the bolts. Their real destiny is to be ballast for the workshop bin liner.

Fit the bolts so that they can catch in slots cut into the carcass, see photo. Stopping the doors can be done in one of a number of ways: before assembly a rebate can be cut in the top rail and solid horizontal member, a strip can be applied top and bottom, or a small stop, like those used for drawers, can be fitted. I chose the latter.

> **Flush bolts fitted to catch in slots in carcass**

SUPPLIERS

Martin & Co., 119 Camden Street, Birmingham B13 DJ tel 0121 233 2111 fax 0121 236 0488

A Japanese c

● **MARK APPLEGATE completed his MSc in Forest Products : Design and Manufacture at Hooke Park College before becoming a self-employed designer-maker. Mark is currently building up his list of clients and would like to fit out his own workshop in the near future**

THE INSPIRATION for this piece evolved over a period of time. I had in mind a design with a simple outline, using striped American black walnut (*Juglans niger*) and some sweet chestnut (*Castanea sativa*) top boards that I'd had for a while. I often get an idea from the timber itself – either the grain pattern, colour, shape, or even a defect, can prove inspirational.

The Japanese element was almost accidental in that I wanted to create a sense of space and air in the piece, and the floating top and uplifting gave it this kind of form.

As it was an exhibition piece, rather than a commission, I was free to design something that I could later use at home.

Sequence

Most of the work in the table and cabinet uses traditional mortice and tenon techniques. All edge joints

"As it was an exhibition piece, rather than a commission, I was free to design something that I could later use at home"

are glued butt joints, the exception being ply tongues, which were used on the top.

After allowing the timber to acclimatise in the workshop I set about machining to size and marking out. I tackled the mortice and tenon joints first. The end frames are the usual single mortice and tenons, while the longitudinal rails have twin tenons which give greater gluing area on this kind of section. I cut all of these using the morticer and table saw. The legs and rails, which receive the panels, were grooved using a router. A table saw could not be used easily for this as some of the grooves are stopped.

Top and panels

The next step is to prepare all panels and horizontal surfaces. Care needs to be taken in proportioning the strips to match the adjacent surfaces. All the joints between the sweet chestnut and American black walnut are shot with a sharp plane before gluing. This ensures that the joint is clearly defined and gap-free – this is time-consuming but well worth the effort!

A point to note about panels and their design is that their width, if possible, should suit the blade or bed size of the planer-thicknesser because, after gluing, they can be re-surfaced and thicknessed easily.

RIGHT: Although construction is straightforward, subtle detailing can transform the design

upboard

A sweet chestnut and
American black walnut
table and cabinet made
by **Mark Applegate**

PHOTOGRAPHY BY STEPHEN HEPWORTH   MAIN ILLUSTRATIONS BY IAN HALL

If this is possible, all grain directions should align correctly. I mark an arrow on the surfaces indicating grain direction, as this can save a lot of time later trying to plane, scrape and sand break-out or torn grain.

The top, shelves, and back panel are too wide for most machines, and these are flattened by hand. Using a router and router table, the panels are then rebated to fit in the grooves in the legs and rails.

Tenons

Next, the tenons, which receive the top, are cut – and the wedges are cut at the same time.

To keep a check on sequence, especially near gluing-up time, I often list operations that need doing. On this job they consist of: slots for the buttons on the top rail, drilling of holes on the legs for adjustable shelf fittings, shaping on the legs, and sanding.

Glue-up

The ends can then be glued-up, making sure that they're kept square and out of wind. After the glue has set, the frames of the end panels can be flushed with a plane, if necessary, to square up the mortice shoulders and prepare for receiving the longitudinal rails and back panel. Again, the cabinet needs to be kept true, but the back panel will help keep the back square.

If, on gluing-up, the legs rock, these can be adjusted by moving the sash cramps slightly to bring one or two of the legs down.

Once set, the bottom shelf can be spot-glued in place and the shelf fitted – probably the most awkward step in the process.

The shelf is marked around the legs and cut out, and the front mitre cut slightly over size. A trial and error process with a sharp chisel will ensure a tight fit on the mitres. The uplift on the shelf can now be planed, across the grain first, and finished along the grain. The shelf is fixed with buttons in the usual way to allow for any movement.

Gentle uplifting on the top, mirrored in the shelf below, helps make the piece less visually heavy

Chamfering on the legs and the shelf, meets with a mitre – a simple but subtle detail

> "The handles are made from American black walnut, mirroring the angles featured on the front"

ABOVE: The same American black walnut features on the back, top sides, and door panels

Fitting the top

The top mortices are marked out carefully from the tenons, and the waste removed with a router. The mortice and wedge room are cleaned up with a chisel to facilitate a clean joint. The top uplift is achieved by the same method as the shelf, but with a lot more planing time.

Once scraped and sanded, the top can be glued to the legs. I find the tone when driving in wedges is satisfying but, when the wedges are decorative, they must be knocked in evenly.

A CRITICAL EYE

When a piece of furniture that I have designed and made is finished, my critical eye inspects it carefully. I assess the design, workmanship, features, and cost. If the piece holds together and the integrity of the design is enhanced by the workmanship and timber, then I deem it to be a successful project.

My feelings about this piece are that, if I were to make it again, I would make some small alterations, but on the whole I am pleased with it. I would not do the light chamfering around the panels again, but would just take off the arris, which would enhance the simplicity of the design.

I always check timber movement – effective drying and acclimatisation in the workshop is important. In this case, the top is held flat by four wedged tenons, which do not normally allow movement. The top has stayed flat and true and the movement has been minimal.

In terms of cost, design features can prove expensive – they are generally worked by hand and so cost more to produce than the whole of the jointing. Complicated features, say on a batch production, could be made by using jigs, but on one-off commissions, the time taken up in producing jigs can take longer than tackling the feature by hand. On the other hand, features should not be rushed, because it is they that will give the piece its integrity – and will also help to sell it! I have found in the past that a lot of people who view furniture do not notice the strong, accurate joints, except perhaps the dovetails, but will notice and comment on design features, the timber, and the final stain, or type of finish!

All these things have to be considered from the outset if a successful piece is to be achieved.

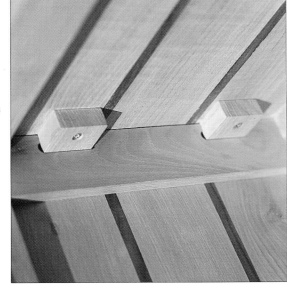

"When a
piece of
furniture
that I have
designed and
made is
finished, my
critical eye
inspects it
carefully"

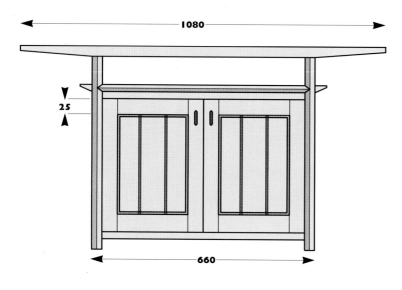

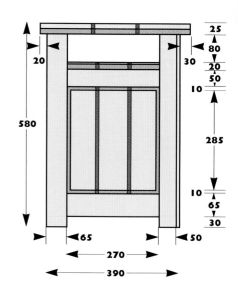

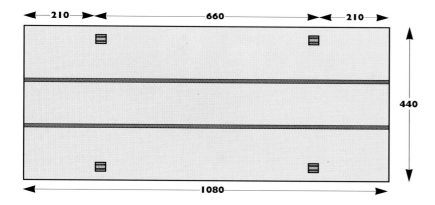

"Features should not be rushed, because it is they that will give the piece its integrity – and will also help to sell it!"

Shelf and doors

RIGHT: American black walnut handles reflecting the chamfer detail on the shelf

The cabinet is now ready to receive the shelf and doors. The shelf is a simple matter of placing on the adjustable brass pegs, and the doors are made in the same way as the end panels. Generally I make doors a spot-on fit for the height, which will require a light touch on the plane for fit, but the width, I make 1 to 2mm (¹⁄₁₆in) over-size to ensure a good fit. Often the meeting stiles will need adjustment once hung on the hinges.

The handles are made from American black walnut, mirroring the angles featured on the front. These are morticed into the stiles.

Final finishing

Now the table and cabinet are scrutinised for any tool marks, chip outs, or torn grain and lightly sanded, finishing with a 400 grit paper.

The whole piece has three coats of pre-catalysed matt cellulose lacquer and is ready for use! ▪

18 FURNITURE-MAKING PROJECTS

Musical chair

John Royall designs and makes a chair for a musician

● **JOHN ROYALL** has recently completed his final year in furniture-making and design at Shrewsbury College of Arts and Technology under Hugh Scriven. He is now taking commissions

RIGHT: A chair for flute and recorder player

BELOW: Turned stretcher rails give support to back

WHEN A MUSICIAN friend asked me to design and make a chair for her own personal use, and to incorporate into its design a representation of her musical lifestyle, my first thought was how to come up with a practical chair, and yet still make it special to herself.

After many designs and cardboard models, I arrived at what I thought could be the solution – a chair which fulfilled all the necessary requirements of stability, rigidity, and comfort, and yet hinted at musicality (*see fig 1*).

I envisaged these facets being expressed in the turned components, these to suggest woodwind instruments. My friend plays flute and recorder, and I even thought of drilling holes in the rails to represent finger holes; however, not wishing to go over the top, I resisted this temptation – for the time being anyway.

Initially I had thought of using rosewood (*Dalbergia sp*) or blackwood (*Acacia melanoxylon*) for the chair as many woodwind instruments are made from these two materials, but as the price of these timbers would have greatly increased the cost of the chair's

construction, I decided ash (*Fraxinus sp*) or oak (*Quercus robur*) would be an acceptable second choice, both being readily available from timber suppliers.

In the end, I settled for ash, not only for its reasonable price but also because of its workability and good laminating possibilities.

Laminated legs

Start with what is by far the lengthiest part of the project – making the laminated curved legs. A curve with a radius of 550mm (22in) is required on the former, which is made from several pieces of 15mm chipboard glued together to accept the width and

length of the laminates.

First finish one piece to the exact required shape, for use as a template. The other pieces are then cut out on the bandsaw, and all are glued together, the sawn pieces being left slightly proud of the template. Use a spindle moulder or hand router to finish the former to the exact curve.

Drill the former at intervals to accept the cramps, at least 50mm (2in) in from the curved edge and approximately 120mm (4¾in) apart, *see fig 2*. Drilling them too close together makes tightening of the cramps difficult, while too wide a spacing does not give adequate distribution of pressure.

PHOTOGRAPHY BY
TIM ROBERTS

19

> "Cascamite must be mixed to its correct consistency – something resembling double cream – otherwise glue failure could occur"

The laminates can now be cut out on the bandsaw and finished to size on the thicknesser, ensuring that enough waste is left on the laminates to account for the considerable cleaning up required after removing from the former.

Cutting laminates

My personal method for cutting laminates is to cut the first piece from the planed stock on the bandsaw, and then to re-plane the sawn surface of the stock ready to cut the next piece, and so forth.

When all the laminates are cut, the sawn faces can be passed through the thicknesser to achieve the correct size. Mark the stock for the edge of the cut laminates before cutting the components. The pieces can then be matched when assembled to ensure the grain runs the same way.

Glue choice

The type of glue used for laminating comes down to personal preference. PVA is fine, but does not allow a lot of time and tends to creep.

I nearly always use Cascamite in this situation, not only for its stability but also because it leaves no glue line. A word of warning though: Cascamite must be mixed to its correct consistency – something resembling double cream – otherwise glue failure can occur.

Before assembling the legs, place paper between the job and the former to avoid unwanted adhesion. Placing a substantial piece of wood – birch-faced ply would be fine – between the

cramps and the laminates helps to distribute the pressure, obviating difficult to remove dents in the work where the cramps were tightened.

With the glued laminates in position, the cramps can now be tightened. Start from the centre of the curve and work towards the ends, gradually bending the laminates around the former as the nuts on the cramps are tightened, *see fig 2*.

> "Before assembling the legs, place paper between the job and the former to avoid unwanted adhesion"

Turning rails

While the laminates are in the cramps, the three rails can be turned on the lathe. The front rail is straightforward enough, but the timber for the two backrest rails must be perfectly square at the outset, the reason being that these are turned so that a square-section centre block is left.

This block provides a good gluing surface for the backrest fixing. The block can be planed into a hexagonal section before assembly.

The front legs, bottom rails and seat rail are all constructed using traditional shouldered mortice and tenon joints, with a haunched mortice and tenon on the seat rail.

ABOVE: Full-size mock-up used at home to test out the practical reality of the design

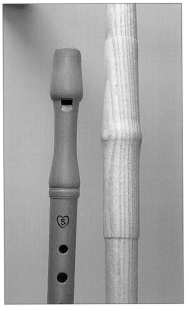

LEFT: Design influence behind the front stretcher rail

LEFT: Tage Frid former for laminating legs

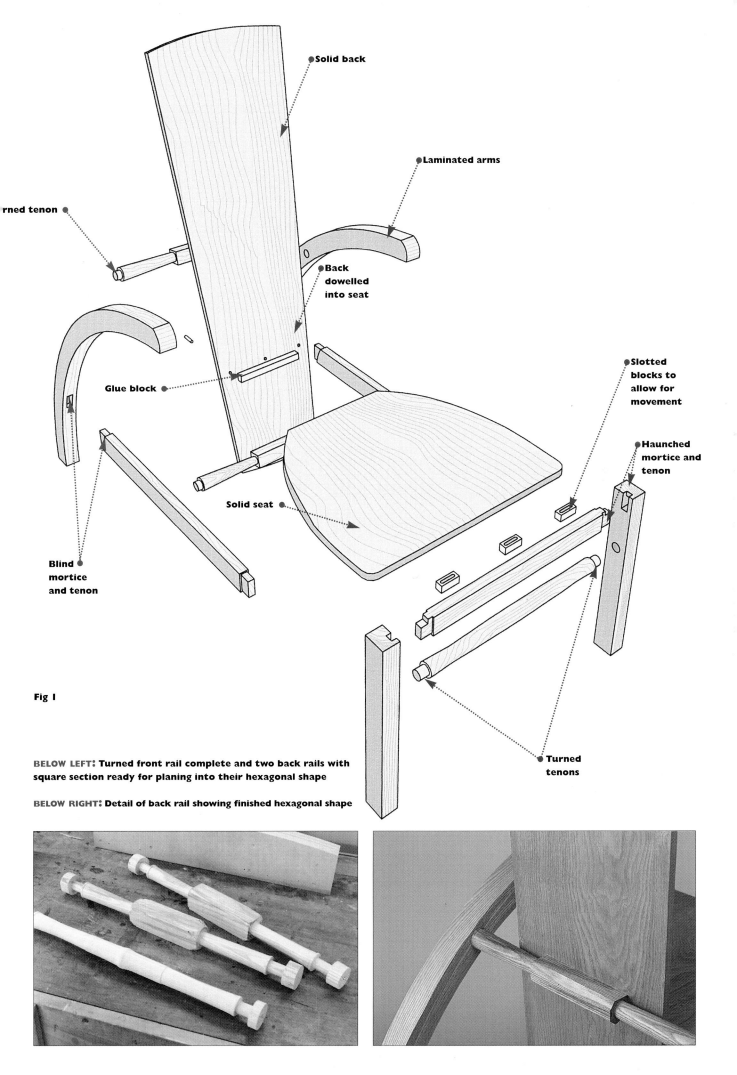

Solid back

Laminated arms

rned tenon

Back
dowelled
into seat

Slotted
blocks to
allow for
movement

Haunched
mortice and
tenon

Glue block

Solid seat

Blind
mortice
and tenon

Fig 1

Turned
tenons

**BELOW LEFT: Turned front rail complete and two back rails with
square section ready for planing into their hexagonal shape**

BELOW RIGHT: Detail of back rail showing finished hexagonal shape

Marking out is straightforward, but care is needed in achieving the curve on the shoulders of the rear tenon on the bottom rail. This can be marked directly from the rod, *see panel*. After cutting out the joints, the front legs, front rail and seat rail can now be glued and cramped up separately.

Rail positioning

The positioning of the two turned rails determines the backrest angle, and so careful working out is required – plus a confidence in one's rod.

It is advisable to make a simple cardboard backrest which can then be temporarily fixed into position to achieve this important angle.

When sure, the mortices for the turned rails can be drilled out on the pillar drill. The legs, bottom rails and turned rails can now be glued and cramped to the chair front section.

I was fortunate in finding a piece of ash which enabled me to cut the backrest as one component. First, cut out the shape on the bandsaw, and then finish with a spokeshave and cabinet scraper.

The backrest can now be glued to the blocks on the turned rails.

"The front of the seat is held in position by three ash blocks glued to the seat rail, and slotted to allow for any movement"

Seat

The seat is made from three pieces of ash, glue-jointed together to provide the width prior to cutting out the shape on a bandsaw. As with the backrest, finish off the seat shape with a spokeshave and scraper.

The front of the seat is held in position by three ash blocks glued to the seat rail, and slotted to allow for any movement, 50mm, 8 gauge screws being used to fix the seat to the blocks.

The rear of the seat is fixed to the backrest by a glue block. Allow 24 hours for the glue to bond, and then insert dowels

MODEL, MOCK-UPS AND RODS

How the design evolved

I generally make several models of an intended piece of furniture, usually at 1:5 scale taken from the design sketches. In my opinion these give a better idea of what the finished piece will look like, and any technical problems arising in the making stage are made far easier to envisage with a scale model than with sketches.

A scale drawing is essential, and I prefer to construct a rod from this, using it as a reference for the making procedure of a piece of furniture.

To give me the exact ergonomic and anthropometric measurements needed for this chair, I decided that a full-scale mock-up of the chair was necessary. This was made from off-cuts and pieces of scrap screwed and bolted together – it's always advisable to construct mock-ups using screws and knock-down fittings, as this makes any adjustments that are required far easier to achieve than for a glued-up model.

I used the mock-up at home for a few days, and this soon told me what alterations had to be made.

through the backrest and into the end-grain of the seat for added strength.

To achieve this, lift slivers of wood along the grain with a chisel, but avoid breaking off the slivers. Drill into the end-grain of the seat and glue the dowels into position.

TOP: Adjustable bevel being used to establish backrest angle in relation to turned rails

ABOVE: Cardboard template helps to finalise exact angle

BELOW: Backrest glued and clamped into position

BELOW: Slotted blocks and glue block on backrest to fix seat

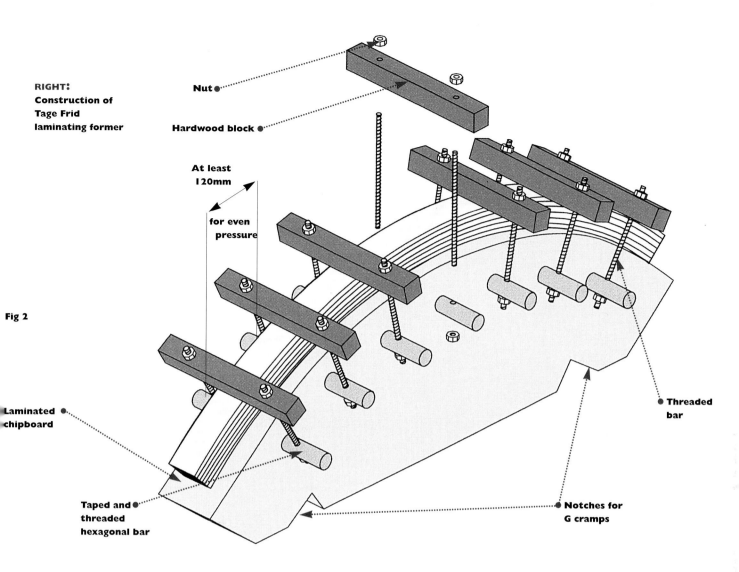

RIGHT:
Construction of
Tage Frid
laminating former

Nut

Hardwood block

At least
120mm

for even
pressure

Fig 2

Laminated
chipboard

Taped and
threaded
hexagonal bar

Threaded
bar

Notches for
G cramps

The slivers of wood can now be glued back down. Great care is required in achieving an acceptable finish using this method. Alternatively, the dowels may be left visible as a decorative feature.

Cleaning up, finishing

I always use the minimum of sanding in the final cleaning up stage, as I prefer the finish that is obtained with a cabinet scraper. The turned rails may, however, need some sanding while on the lathe, and the sharp edges can be removed from the chair by using

00 grade sandpaper.

Finishing is wide and varied, and depends upon personal preference. For this project I wanted to keep the wood quite light, and so a single coat of danish oil followed by two coats of finishing wax completed the job.

My friend has assured me that she is pleased with her chair, and uses it constantly for home music sessions; so pleased in fact, that I think I heard her mumbling something about wanting a musician's desk to complement her chair. Now where did I put that former…?

> "I think I heard her mumbling something about wanting a musician's desk to complement her chair"

VACUUM FORMING VERSUS BENDING

The two most common methods used in the lamination of wood are the more recent vacuum forming, and the traditional method of bending the laminates around a former with the use of cramps.

Vacuum forming is where the glued laminates and the former are placed together in position in an airtight rubber bag. The air is then removed from the bag, forcing the laminates to conform to the desired shape.

The advantage of this method is that even pressure is

maintained all round. One of the disadvantages is that any movement occurring inside the bag during the process cannot be seen from the outside.

Everything must, therefore, be in place and unlikely to move before the vacuum is created.

I have had good results using this method on smaller laminating projects, but in this instance I decided to use the Tage Frid method of clamping the laminates to the former, see *main text.*

In harmony

PHOTOGRAPHY BY TIM ROBERTS

John Royall makes a desk to go with his musician's chair

"What I was aiming for was a simple, uncomplicated desk, light enough to be moved around a room with ease"

LEFT: A musical table to compliment a musical chair

BELOW: The original chair and table together

I HAVE ALWAYS found it satisfying to see two pieces of furniture that come together and complement each other. Many different pieces can co-exist well enough together, but to produce two pieces that visually belong to each other is a challenge – and very rewarding when they are successful. The client who commissioned my Musician's Chair, *see previous article*, asked me if I could design and make her a small desk to go with it, and I readily agreed.

As with the chair, design sketches and scale models soon started to accumulate. Some helped to fill up the waste paper basket, while others became possibilities and found their way onto the shelf in the workshop.

What I was aiming for was a simple, uncomplicated desk, light enough to be moved around a room with ease, yet providing a substantial writing surface and storage facility for A3 and A4 musical notation sheets.

Design priority

The laminated curve used in the chair's construction was a standard priority design feature from the outset. The task was to design the desk's work surface around the curved legs. Initially I had envisaged a single shallow drawer for the storage area, but I settled for an open shelf design. When I was satisfied with the final model, I started the making procedure.

I still had an ample supply of ash, *fraxinus excelsior*, left from the chair project, and so there was no need for a trip to the timber merchant.

The method for producing the curved legs is the same procedure I used for the chair, using a former and Tage Frid clamps, but there is an adjustment needed, *see panel.*

Whilst the laminates are glued and clamped, the back legs can be cut and planed to size. For extra strength I decided to use a double mortise & tenon for fixing the leg components together. This is a good joint – and, with a little time and trouble in the making, it doubles the amount of side-grain to side-grain contact, ensuring a very secure fixing.

> "The task was to design the desk's work surface around the curved legs"

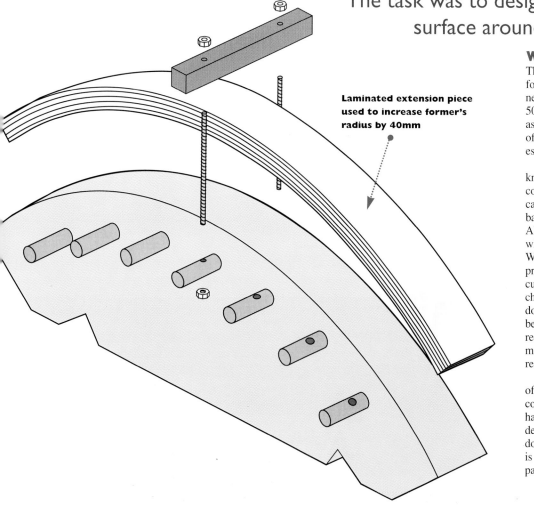

Laminated extension piece used to increase former's radius by 40mm

Worktop

The front, back, and side components for the desk worktop can be made next. I left the back component 50mm (2in) wider, so when the top is assembled this forms a lip on the rear of the work surface and stops the escape of rolling pens and pencils.

I decided to use finger joints, also known as box joints, in the construction of the desktop. These can be cut out fairly quickly on the bandsaw and tidied up by hand. Alternatively a router can be used with the appropriate straight cutter. When set up, each joint can be produced by one or two passes of the cutter. One point to remember when choosing finger joints is that, unlike dovetails which usually only need to be cramped one way, this joint will require pressure in both directions, so make sure plenty of sash cramps are ready to hand.

It is advisable to cut out the shape of the shelf-opening in the front component after the finger joints have been made, but before the desktop is assembled. This can be done on the bandsaw. A spokeshave is then the best tool to complete this part of the job

HIDE TO NOTHING

Adhesives are many and varied and I did some test pieces using several different glues to find the most suitable. Impact adhesive is fine, but make sure you get it right first time or you're in trouble – any adjustments are virtually impossible.

There are spray adhesives available for fixing vinyl and other plastic materials but over large areas I found them less successful. In the end I used PVA wood glue. It gave a firm fixing, and did not react in any way with the vinyl. Another advantage is that it gives you a little more time to make any necessary adjustments. It is possible to place the covered component into a veneer press, but be careful not to over tighten as this could crush the vinyl and leave thin areas. Alternatively weights can be placed on a piece of MDF or plywood.

I will mention here that the use of vinyl as a covering was not a personal choice. My client is a vegan and the use of any animal hide was not be acceptable to her. However some very good synthetic materials are available and of course they cost considerably less than leather. Different glues may be needed if you do use leather.

> "It is easier to fit the desktop to the leg components, before fitting the work surface into its frame, than visa versa"

Interior shelf

Stub mortise and tenons are used to fix the interior shelf sides to the front and back of the desktop. Groove the sides first to accept the shelf floor. A dovetail housing is the most efficient method of fixing the shelf back into position. Cut out the housing with a router and dovetail cutter, the tail can be made on the bandsaw and tidied up with a sharp chisel.

The shelf floor is made from 9mm (⅜in) MDF. An ash lipping is attached to the front of the shelf, but make sure that this is left slightly proud of the shelf surface to accommodate the vinyl covering. It is at this stage that it is necessary to cover the shelf floor with the vinyl. Form a rebate along both sides of the floor of which the tongue then locates into the groove in the shelf sides. The shoulder of the rebate makes a good edge for the vinyl to finish against.

Assembly

The next stage is to dry assemble all the desktop components and check everything for square. If satisfied, glue and cramp up the top. Don't forget to make sure that the shelf floor is in position, as it cannot be fitted afterwards. When the cramps are removed the rear of the shelf floor can be screwed into the shelf back, as in a traditional drawer construction.

It is easier to fit the desktop to the leg components, before fitting the work surface into its frame, than vice versa. The legs are glued straight to the sides of the desktop, but I decided that extra fixing was required to ensure rigidity. Normally I would have screwed through the desktop sides and into the legs to achieve this.

ABOVE: To avoid the possibility of splitting the laminates, and to add some mechanical strength to the mating surfaces, knock down fittings were epoxied in place

BELOW LEFT: Curved laminated leg is twin tenoned into back leg, note shaping on the top of the back leg

> "It is advisable to cut out the shape of the shelf-opening in the front component after the finger joints have been made, but before the desktop is assembled"

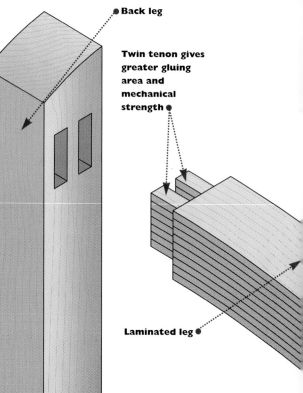

Back leg

Twin tenon gives greater gluing area and mechanical strength

Laminated leg

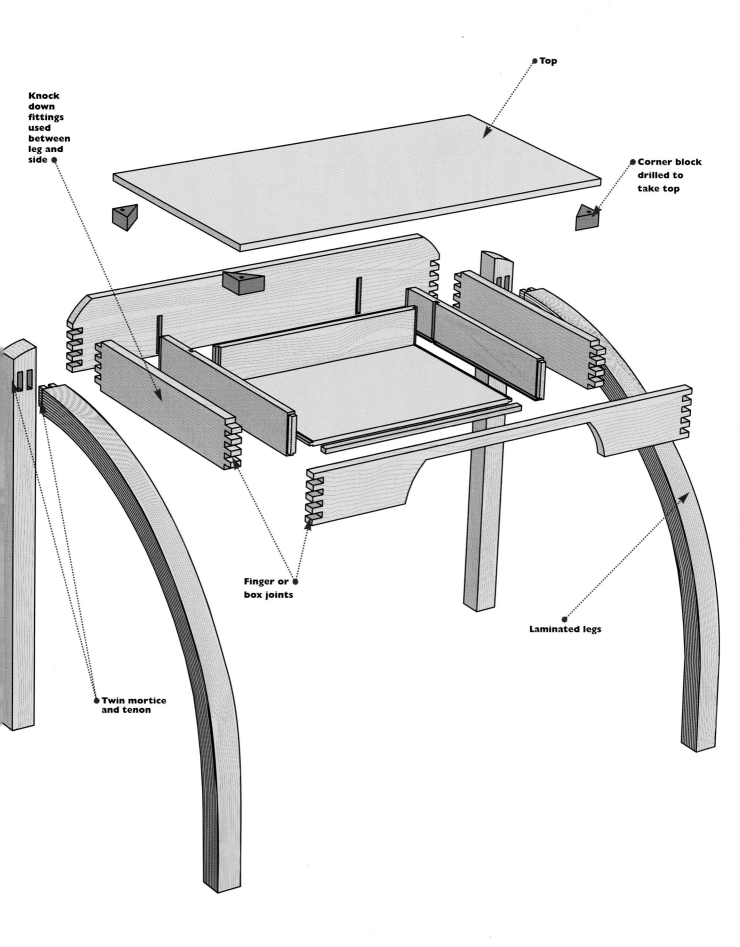

Knock
down
fittings
used
between
leg and
side ●

● Top

● Corner block
drilled to
take top

● Finger or
box joints

● Twin mortice
and tenon

Laminated legs ●

CLAMP REPEAT

The underside of the desk's work-surface has to clear the top of the chair's armrests to enable the chair to be pushed under the desk when not in use. To achieve this the radius of the curve which is 550mm (21⅝in) has to be increased to 590mm (23¼in), a difference of 40mm (1¾in). Two choices are available here – one is to construct a new former with the desired radius, the other is to use the method I employed.

Cut some laminates to the same width as the former, and enough of them to achieve a thickness of 40mm (1¾in) when glued together. These laminates can now be glued and cramped to the former as if making the legs themselves. When completed, this curved piece becomes an extension, increasing the former's radius by the desired amount, and yet maintaining the correct arc, see drawing. The actual laminates for the legs can now be cut on the bandsaw and finished to size in the planer-thicknesser. Clamp the laminates to the former using the same procedure as in the chair project. Although they could be removed much sooner, especially in heated workshop conditions, I personally err on the side of caution and never like to disturb glued-up laminations for a minimum of 24 hours.

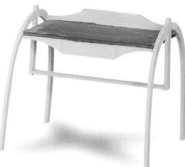

ABOVE: The knock down fittings used to attach the laminated leg to the side of the desk

RIGHT: Several models were made to help visualise the design and envisage any technical problems

BELOW: Internal structure of desk, corner blocks are used to fix the top

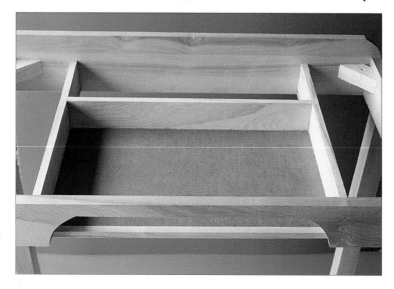

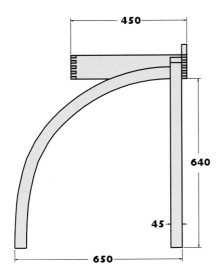

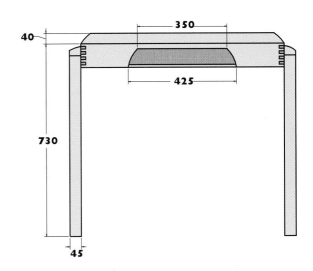

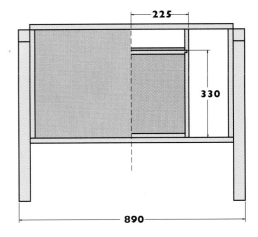

"My client assures me that the desk and chair are the best of friends, and get along together just fine"

However I was concerned that there was a possibility, although small, that the screws may have forced open the laminates, and so I used KD fittings instead. Drill the legs to take the threaded inserts and fix them in position with Araldite. After the top is glued into position, screw into the inserts with machine screws.

I used 12mm (½in) MDF for the work surface, and it is held in position by four ash blocks glued and screwed into the four corners of the worktop frame. It is usual to cut slots for the screws in the blocks to allow for any movement that occurs but, as the MDF will not present this problem, it is not necessary. Set the MDF slightly below the sides of the frame so that when the covering is in place the vinyl will finish flush with the edges of the worktop.

Finally screw the work surface to the blocks using 38mm (1½in) 8 gauge screws.

The finish is exactly the same as for the chair – a generous coat of Danish Oil followed by several coats of wax.

My client assures me that the desk and chair are the best of friends, and get along together just fine. All in all, I think the two pieces compliment each other well. ■

Dressing it up

Have you noticed that most of Editor **Paul Richardson**'s projects are tables with drawers? Here's his excuse

BELOW: A simplified version of a Hepplewhite original

THE MORE 17th and 18th century style furniture I make, the more I am impressed by the versatility of certain standard forms of construction developed over that period. Using these relatively simple conventions as building blocks, designers and craftsmen satisfying the ever-more discerning and demanding market of the Georgian and Regency periods, were able to produce a great diversity of specialised furniture types without having to reinvent the wheel every time.

This freedom from having to consider the fundamentals of how each piece was made must have contributed greatly to the refinement of proportion and decorative treatment that took place over the hundred years or so in question; if it is already known how the piece will be constructed, then more time and imagination can be applied to appearance and detail.

> "This freedom from having to consider the fundamentals of how each piece was made must have contributed greatly to the refinement of proportion and decorative treatment that took place over the hundred years or so in question"

Adaptable

Of these standard forms, none is more adaptable than the table carcass. I seem to have spent half of my working life making pieces that use this simple and reliable arrangement, without feeling at all restricted. Basically anything with legs, a flat surface and a drawer or drawers can be made in this way – Pembroke and library tables are obvious; but bonheur-du-jours, Carlton house desks and all manner of complicated-looking furniture can be made by adding a box-carcass superstructure to the top and adjusting a few details.

Further variety can be added by truncating the legs so that they are merely corner posts, allowing the carcass to be supported on a pedestal base. Some of the most extravagant Regency furniture is made in this way, sofa tables being a good example; end standards, pedestal columns on platform bases, and scroll-form supports with intermediate platforms and Regency knee legs, all being pressed into service.

I made the dressing table shown here several years ago and it is almost as simple as a table carcass gets – made with only one drawer it would be the core building block. In appearance it is based on a Sheraton pattern, the original having a split, hinged top which opens to reveal a fitted interior with mirror rising on an easel. Splendid as this is, the client's budget didn't allow for so much work, so we settled on keeping the proportions but restricting the fitting to two straightforward drawers.

Tapered legs

As, in this construction, all main carcass parts are jointed into the legs, these should be prepared first. Squareness is more than usually important so plane the stock

BELOW: A simplified version of a Hepplewhite original

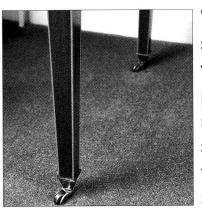

"I seem to have spent half of my working life making pieces that use this simple and reliable arrangement, without feeling at all restricted"

carefully, then form the taper. This starts at the position of the lower drawer rail, and is cut on the two inner faces of each leg only.

Cutting tapers may be done in a number of ways; hand-planing is undemanding in the Brazilian mahogany (*swietania macrophylla*) used here, or jigs may be made for use with a table saw or thicknesser. I use a rather inadvisable technique on an overhand planer which I can't honestly recommend on safety grounds – it is a bad habit that I have fallen into. I hope you're not too shocked.

"Ideally the grain should run through both drawers and the rails, cut from a single pair of veneers, but on a tight budget…"

Boxwood line
If working in rosewood (*dalbergia spp.*) or satinwood (*fagara flava*), the next step would be to veneer the legs. In either case, though, a boxwood (*buxus sempervirens*) line is applied to the arrises, for which a rebate just smaller than the line must be cut. I do this with a router inverted in a table, and find that a closed fence – that is, a false fence through which the cutter is plunged, leaving zero clearance – gives the cleanest result. To further ensure a neat rebate, especially on veneered work, back-feed the material in the direction of the cutter's rotation. Normally this is a bad idea, but in this case the amount of stock removed is so small that, provided a firm grip is maintained, there shouldn't be a problem.

When rebates have been cut in all corners of the legs, glue the line in with PVA, carefully wiping off any surplus and holding in place with taut masking tape until dry. Scrape the line flush.

Next cut a tenon on each leg to fit square socket castors – don't leave it till later as it will be much more difficult when the table is assembled.

Drawer rails
The front of the carcass is archetypal in that it is formed by drawer rails; the uppermost being dovetailed into the top of the legs while the others are tenoned into their inner faces.

Note that the legs are proud of the carcass rails and sides by the thickness of the boxwood line.

I crossbanded the drawer rails to match the drawer fronts – this isn't absolutely necessary as they are mahogany anyway, but is more in period and unifies the front of the piece.

Cut the shoulders of all three drawer rails' joints – and, indeed, the carcass back – at the same time, ensuring that they are exactly the same, or problems will result. Cut mortices in the legs and the tenons to fit, then cut the dovetails on the ends of the top rail.

Transfer these dovetails to the top of their respective legs by marking round them with a knife, then take out the waste with a router, before paring back to the line with a chisel.

The front legs and drawer rails may now be glued up; tenons first then the dovetails.

Biscuits
The back and sides are traditionally tenoned or rabbeted into the legs; here I have used biscuits as the joint is quite long. This allows for a good number of biscuits to be fitted – less than three No. 20s would be inadequate, I feel, but four is plenty in a case such as this where the joints will not be heavily stressed. Over-sized 'proper' joints can be

counter-productive here, as the amount of wood removed to make them weakens the leg; biscuits with high performance modern adhesives are a good balance.

In original examples I have seen drawer runners attached in a number of ways: glued in place with Scotch glue; nailed to the carcass sides – this in an otherwise high-quality Pembroke table – and dovetailed and tenoned into the legs as with the drawer rails.

A larger piece that might be dragged around – a biggish library table, for example – might warrant the extra security of dovetails and tenons, but here the front, sides and back are screwed to the top anyway, and as previously mentioned the legs are easily weakened by the cutting of innumerable mortices and sockets. Restorers are often faced with the repair of a split leg as a result – so once again biscuits are used, joining the runners to the carcass sides. To prevent twisting, the runners are cut round the back legs and pinned into them; at the front they are dowelled into the drawer rails.

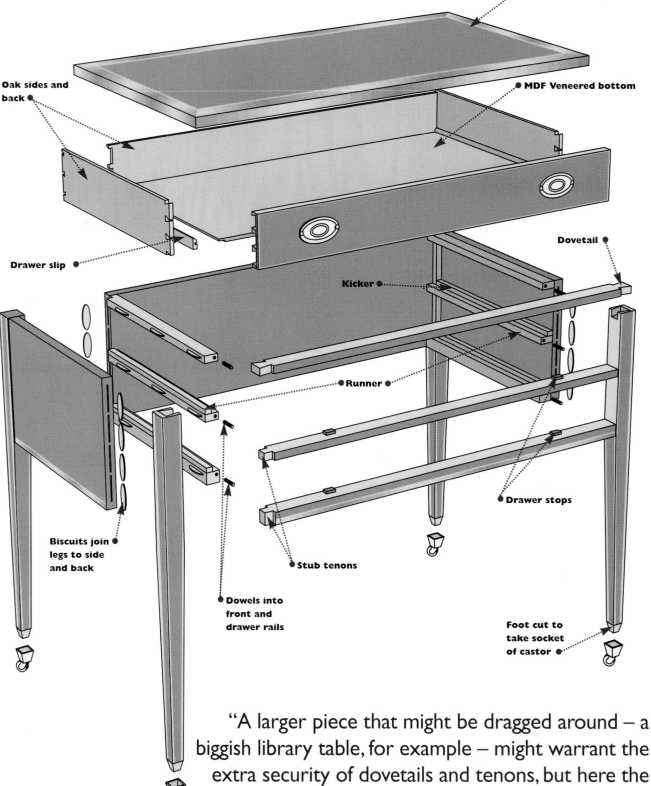

MDF Veneered top

Oak sides and back

MDF Veneered bottom

Drawer slip

Dovetail

Kicker

Runner

Biscuits join legs to side and back

Drawer stops

Stub tenons

Dowels into front and drawer rails

Foot cut to take socket of castor

"A larger piece that might be dragged around – a biggish library table, for example – might warrant the extra security of dovetails and tenons, but here the front, sides and back are screwed to the top anyway"

Assembly

Assembly order is fairly important; the front legs and rails are already glued up, so make up the back and back legs, then glue the runners to the sides. When these are dry complete the carcass by joining back and front with the sides, checking for square.

To give the piece a little visual lift, and to relieve the flatness of the carcass, a bought-in satinwood banding is applied to the lower edges. I use the word 'applied' deliberately as it is literally glued onto the surface, not let into a rebate. Not quite proper, I agree, but I rather like the effect.

Drawers

The drawers are standard issue, being dovetailed with oak (*quercus spp.*)

linings and mahogany fronts – the veneered MDF bottoms are fitted by means of drawer slips. The fronts are veneered with book-matched curl mahogany, the central join lining up with that of the top – ideally the grain should run through both drawers and the rails, cut from a single pair of veneers, but on a tight budget... always veneer drawer fronts after the drawers are made, by the

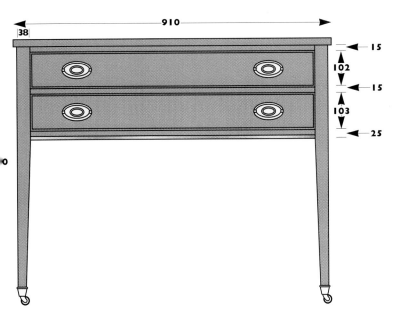

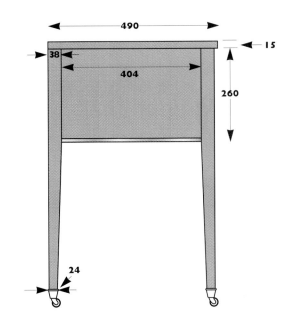

"Lay the crossbanding and line at the same time, working quickly and hammering towards the main veneer"

way – they are almost never veneered with a balancer on their backs, so might move unless restrained by the drawer's construction.

The boxwood line is fitted in the same way as that on the legs, but fit the drawers first to avoid narrowing the line when adjusting their fronts.

The top of this piece is veneered onto a groundwork of MDF, which is highly suitable for Scotch glue veneering, if sanded a little first. The following is a description of the order in which the top is veneered when using Scotch glue and a hammer – if you prefer some other method then skip the next couple of paragraphs and good luck to you.

Veneering
The top is first cut to finished size, then veneered on the reverse with plain mahogany. This balancing veneer is there to prevent the cupping that would otherwise occur if the top was veneered on its top surface only.

Prepare the two leaves of curl mahogany veneer for the top by sponging lightly with very hot water, then pressing between two boards of MDF or chipboard for a few hours. Cut sufficient satinwood crossbanding for the job – a paper-cutting guillotine

is good for this, but a Stanley knife and straight edge will do – again wet it with hot water, and press it in a stack between the jaws of a vice until ready to use.

Trim the curl veneers to about 12mm (½in) shorter than the depth of the top.

Turn the top over, placing newspaper beneath, and mark the centre line onto the MDF with a ballpoint pen. Lay the first veneer with Scotch and a hammer overlapping this line, then the second overlapping the centre line by the same amount – but on the other side, if you see what I mean.

Lay a wooden straight edge along your marked line, and cut through both veneers with a sharp knife. Peel off the waste, and hammer down the join.

Crossbanding
Now; the next step is to trim the laid veneers for the crossbanding. I generally use a sharp cutting gauge for this, running along the edge of the groundwork, but again a wooden straight edge and knife will do. Whichever, cut a perimeter that is slightly smaller in depth than the combined width of your crossbanding and boxwood line. Again peel off the waste.

Lay the crossbanding and line at the same time, working quickly and hammering towards the main veneer. Cut each join by the overlap technique, and when you reach a corner do the same, cutting the mitre through both layers.

The edge is crossbanded in the same way.

Possibilities
This table was bodied-up with amber varnish and given a slightly 'dirty' French polish so that it didn't look too new, and the castors and handles – both from Martin & Co. – were fitted.

This table was quick to make, and I hope that some of the possibilities of building on it are apparent – slightly heavier legs and a glazed superstructure on top as a display cabinet perhaps? Budget permitting, of course. ■

BELOW LEFT:
Oak-veneered MDF drawer bottoms are fitted in slips

BELOW: Apply crossbanding and boxwood line at the same time

Supplier
*Castors and handles from **Martin & Co**, 119 Camden Street, Birmingham, B1 3DJ. Tel 0121 233 2111 or 0121 603 2111 fax 0121 236 0488.*

Starting with dovetails

In the first of a two-part project on making a dressing table mirror, Projects Editor **Colin Eden-Eadon** concentrates on carcass dovetails

ABOVE: An Arts and Crafts toilet mirror – a good exercise in carcass and drawer dovetailing

JOY IS the opportunity to mix business with pleasure, like making this Arts & Crafts-style toilet mirror and drawer within the familiar confines of my timber-built garden workshop, from which I can take in glorious views of the Essex countryside.

I'm the first to admit that I'm luckier than some. At 18ft by 25ft, my workshop is a little bigger than most – and, as my wife is wont to remind me, is marginally larger than our living room!

This piece is designed to be made by woodworkers seeking to advance their skills, and uses tools I have in my own workshop – a bandsaw, a planer-thicknesser, a table-mounted router, my small Multico PM 12 morticer with drilling attachment, plus planes and chisels.

If, however, some of the machinery is not available, don't feel this project must be rejected, as most of the processes involved can be tackled with a router or by hand.

Materials

I chose American white oak (*Quercus alba*) for the main carcass. Brazilian mahogany (*Swietenia macrophylla*) for the drawer sides and English walnut (*Juglans regia*) for the feet and handles provide a pleasing contrast to the oak.

Machine up all the stock material for the carcass first and leave over-thickness, resting the wood under weights for a few days before planing to final thickness. This is particularly important with American white oak which is prone to honeycombing – a defect rather like a shake due to poor kilning.

ABOVE: No cross-cut saw? Use a shooting board to square the ends of carcass components

ABOVE: As the ends of the carcass joints are mitred, the back's rebate can be run through. Here a table-mounted router is used, but a rebate plane would do as well

ABOVE: Marking the carcass dovetails using a home-made wooden block and a pencil sharpened to a chisel point. Note the hatching of the waste area to be cut out

ABOVE: Marking the mitre

ABOVE: Marking pins from tails – note the weight holding things in position and the double-ended, alternate bevel marking knife

Main carcass

Having prepared the carcass material, the pieces can be cut to length and width. I have no powered cross-cut saw so I am a devotee of the shooting board.

Mark to length and scribe around with a marking knife, then cut on the bandsaw close to the line, planing to it on the shooting board. Before preparing to mark out the dovetails, drawer stop mortices must be cut into the front edge of the bottom piece of the carcass – a job which will be impossible once the carcass is glued up, *see drawing*.

This can be accomplished with either a hollow chisel morticer or a router, cleaned out with a chisel.

Next, mark the carcass thickness for the dovetails. I allow an extra 1mm (³⁄₆₄in) of thickness to allow for cleaning up on both the tails and the pins. I then mark round all the pieces with a marking gauge.

Before marking out the dovetails, rebates for the back need to be considered. I wanted to avoid stopped rebates where possible, so I chose to use mitres as this allows the rebate for the back to be cut all the way through.

For continuity's sake I put a mitre on the front as well as the back.

Dovetails

Talk to individual makers and they will probably have their own idiosyncratic methods of marking out and cutting dovetails. Take the old chestnut of whether to do tails or pins first: I am a tails first man, partly because it was the way I was taught and also because it seems to me to have logical sequence.

As to setting out, some makers will be extremely mathematical and precise, others will rely completely on judgement by eye. My own method is a combination of the two: I consider the number of tails that I think will both look pleasing and also fit the width of the carcass.

Having decided that five dovetails fitted this particular bill, I divided the width of the carcass by five (165mm minus 12mm for the back rebate and the front mitre). This leaves 153mm, which divided by 5 equals 30.6mm. This space is equivalent to one tail and half a pin.

Mark these on the wood and square a line down on each of the marks. Next, decide what size the pin is to be. I would advise against making it too small if these are a first attempt at dovetails.

Another consideration at this juncture is chisel size; there's no point deciding on delicate pins only to discover the lack of a chisel small enough to clean them up with.

Marking out

Using a dovetail marker or a sliding bevel, mark out half a pin on each side of the line. Repeat this process until all five marks have a complete pin.

I like to use an H or 2H pencil with a chisel point for certain types of marking out. I mark out the tails in pencil then, if a mistake is made, an ugly knife line does not mar the work; a little wander off the original line will probably not show.

Mark the waste area of the pins with hatching to avoid any confusion – people have been known to cut out the wrong piece…

Cut the tails of each side individually or, if feeling really brave, cramp the two together and cut in one go.

With a coping saw, cut out the waste. I then like to remark the gauged line in the shoulder area of the pins by taking a square and

ABOVE: Chopping out the pins – note the angle at which the chisel is held; doing this from both faces leaves a 'hill'

BELOW: Paring the 'hill' flat and square to the face

BOTTOM: Testing the fit. Don't dry-fit dovetails any further than this or they may be damaged when taken apart

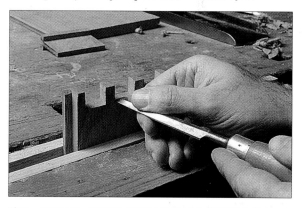

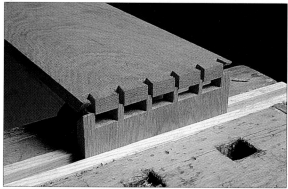

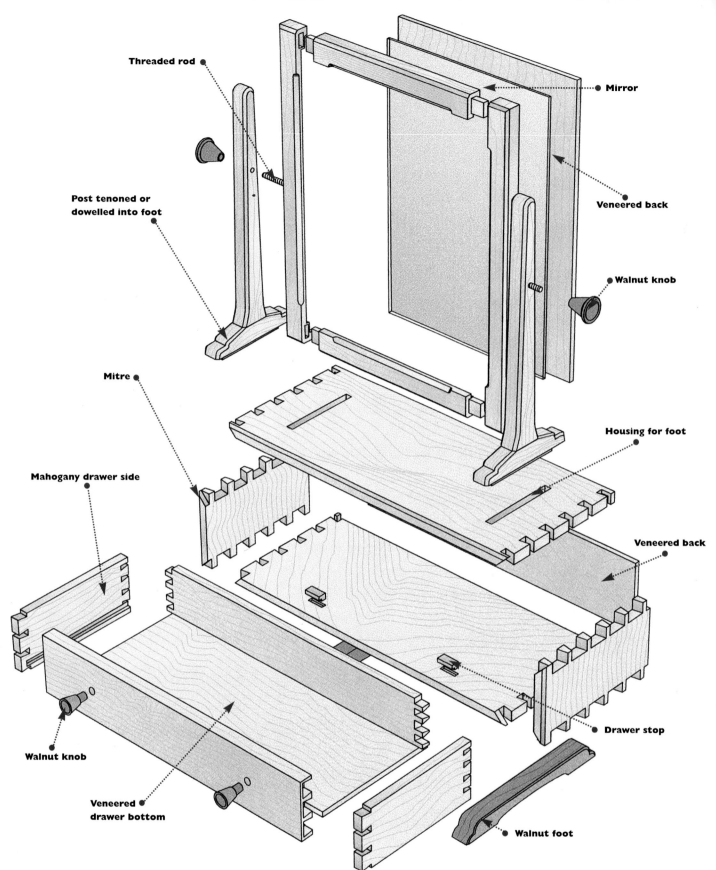

Threaded rod

Post tenoned or
dowelled into foot

Mitre

Mahogany drawer side

Walnut knob

Veneered
drawer bottom

Mirror

Veneered back

Walnut knob

Housing for foot

Veneered back

Drawer stop

Walnut foot

knifing the lines again, *see photo*.

Set up the piece in bench dogs or cramp to the bench with a couple of G cramps.

Place the correctly sized chisel on the knife line and then chop with a mallet at a slight angle. This will cut to the line, leaving a slight 'hill' in the middle.

Turn the work over and repeat from the other side. Being a lazy person, I do the next stage sitting down. While some

people prefer to do their paring on the bench, I am more comfortable seated, and in a better position to see what I am doing. Clamp one piece in the vice and pare down until the hill in the middle that was created in each pin socket is flat – check this with a square.

Mitres, tail sockets

Mitres, which are fitted more easily after the dovetails are cut,

are now marked and sawn near to the line.

Find a piece of scrap that is about the length of the carcass and 50mm (2in) in thickness, setting it level with one of the side pieces in the vice. Place the relevant carcass piece on top with a heavy weight to stop it moving, and carefully scribe the tails, *see photo*.

Repeat this process for each piece and square down with a

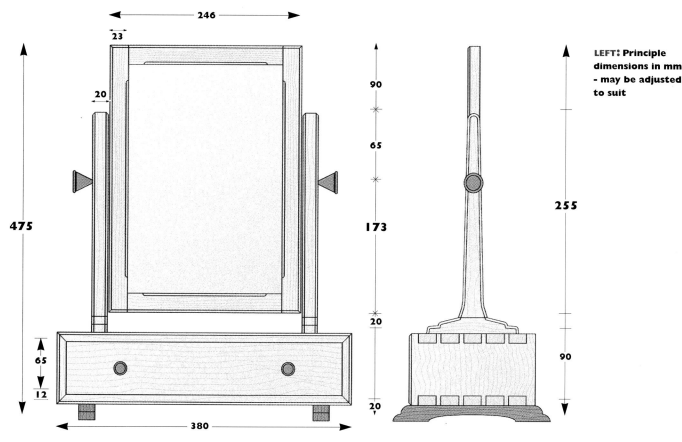

246

23

20

475

65

12

380

90

65

173

20

20

255

90

knife. These lines can be difficult to see, especially for those of us with poor eyesight. This is where a sharp 2H pencil comes in; running the point in the knife line highlights and clarifies it.

Again, hatch the waste areas to be cut out and re-mark the shoulder areas of the sockets with a knife. Saw right up against the waste side of the line, then cut out the socket middles with a coping saw. Clean up using the same process as before.

Check for fit by tapping the joint – gently – part-way together with a hammer and block. Tapping all the way is a little risky with small cross-grained pieces; these can be difficult to separate because there is so little to hold on to.

They should be a tight fit, but not so tight that a sledgehammer is required! Pare very carefully back to the knife lines to correct any wander.

The mitres can now be fitted and trued up.

Applying finish

Make life easier by cleaning up all inside surfaces now rather than when the piece is assembled, and apply your preferred finish.

As with any gluing-up operation, preparation is the key to success. I always prepare some sash cramps to the right size even if I do not eventually use them. They can be very useful just for the final little squeeze needed to pull up a joint.

Cutting some cramping blocks with cut-outs the same size as the tails will help to maximise the cramp pressure if necessary. I also find that covering the bench top with a melamine-faced board provides an easy wipe-down surface that can be bashed around and generally abused in the controlled calmness of every glue-up.

In the next article Colin describes how he made the drawer, mirror frame, posts and feet

TUNING UP

Good lighting will improve the chances of success with dovetail cutting. An anglepoise light over the back of the bench will help considerably when it comes to peering through pins and tails.

Some of the tools used for marking out dovetails can be tuned up in a number of ways to improve their performance.

Most marking gauges come with a round pin that extends too far from the stock. This not only makes for awkward use, but also produces a very scratchy line. I was taught to knock the pin back until only about 3mm protrudes. By carefully

sharpening this to a chisel point a clean cutting action allows accurate knife-like marking out.

For most marking out my personal preference is a Japanese knife. However, when scribing dovetails I use a home-made knife that is ground with the opposite bevel on each end.

This is because although slightly ambidextrous, I do find scribing the left-hand side of a dovetail difficult with a marking knife that has the bevel on the right-hand side. A double-ended reversible knife made from a piece of old bandsaw or hacksaw blade solves this problem.

Another useful aid is a home-made dovetail template made from various materials. Mine is from an offcut of oak, but thin sheet metal, brass or even one milled out of solid metal would suffice.

Mirror finish

PHOTOGRAPHY BY MICHAEL MANNI

With the dovetailed carcass accomplished, Projects Editor **Colin Eden-Eadon** moves on to complete his mirror

THE DIFFICULTY of the first part of this project, *see page 34*, was in the dovetailing for the carcass. The concluding stage, which covers making the drawers, frame and posts for this American white oak (*Quercus alba*) and English walnut (*Juglans regia*) toilet mirror, depends for success on careful planning as the mirror frame must be made first, so that the drilling position of the posts which take the pivot holes can be set up.

> "Gluing up and sliding in the drawer bottom helps to keep the piece in square"

Drawers

Make up the components of the drawers and carefully fit to length and width. Some makers like to put an imperceptible bevel on the edges and tops and bottoms of the drawer front to produce a tight fit; this can be eased by planing once the drawer is glued up.

Another useful tip is to sink the tails a fraction deeper, 0.5mm at the most; this allows minimal fitting of the Brazilian mahogany (*Swietenia macrophylla*) drawer sides without having to plane off surplus material.

RIGHT: The 'real thing' transferred from the drawing

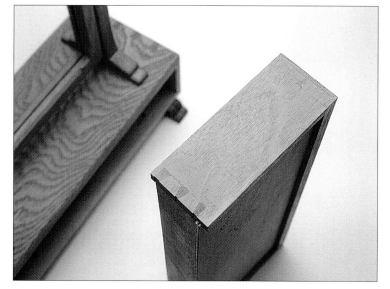

> "This is another example of where setting up a router in a table is easier than using a fence"

Set out on the bench and mark up the pieces, matching pins to tails. Decide how many tails to have on the front and back and mark out as for the carcass dovetails, noting that the number of back tails and pins depends on the depth of the drawer back; this in turn depends on the position of the drawer bottom groove.

Next, cut out the tails and mark out the pins. To cut out the waste on the drawer front, a router can be used freehand, but by the time the power tool has been set up this job can probably be done as quickly by hand. Clean up and fit.

For two reasons the grooves are best machined on a router table: firstly, for safety because the components are fairly small; secondly, this method gives more control and avoids having to mess around with awkward fences and run-off blocks.

The two side grooves should be stopped to safeguard the front of the tail.

To prevent problems later, drill the holes in the drawer front for the walnut knobs.

For both the backs and the drawer bottom I used 6mm veneered ply. These could also be made out of solid timber if desired. Gluing up and sliding in the drawer bottom helps to keep the piece in square.

The drawer stops are now fitted. These are a small rebated section, *see drawing*, that allows the depth in which the drawer is set to be adjusted. This is achieved by taking small amounts off the stops, either with a shoulder plane once they are glued in, or by planing to fit before gluing.

Mirror frame

The frame can either be tenoned or dowelled together; whichever technique is used, mark out with enough space to allow for the double rebate for the back and the mirror.

Cut the mortices on a small portable morticer and the tenon on a table-mounted router, using a cross-slide with a false fence to avoid spelching.

Mark the shoulders of the tenons with a knife; this will also help avoid break-out. Alternatively, they can be cut on a bandsaw or even by hand.

The mirror glass and the back are set into the double rebate which must be stopped on the longer of the two frame pieces.

The first rebate is the 4mm depth of the mirror glass, and 7mm wide. If the glass is cut a little narrower then small wedges can be inserted on either side to hold the mirror in place.

The second rebate is the same 6mm depth as the back and 9mm wide to allow space for the screws.

The corners of the rebates can be cleaned up square with a chisel. This is another example of where setting up a router in a table is easier than using a fence.

For the chamfers on the inside and outside of the frame I used a chamfer cutter set up in the router, but this job can be done by hand with a chisel bevel down and a spokeshave. The outside chamfer can be planed around – sometimes as quick – but in this instance because the chamfer is the same as the internal one it can be accomplished using the same setting.

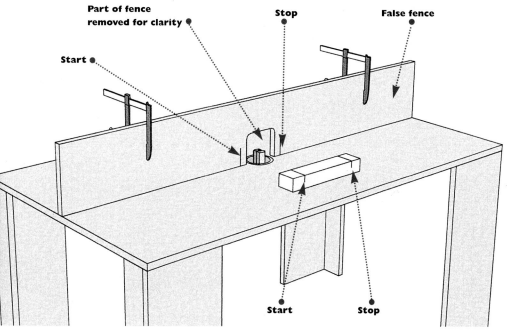

Part of fence
removed for clarity

Start

Stop

False fence

Start

Stop

Fig 1: Set-up for stopped rebates on a router table

Knobs

My father turned the knobs for the drawers and mirror frame in walnut to match the feet. The threaded part of the knob mechanism for the mirror is made from an M5 chrome nut and bolt.

The nut is epoxy-glued into the base of the knob, the hole which takes the thread being drilled a little deeper to allow for tightening.

The other end of the bolt is cut off and the length worked out for the remaining piece. This is best done by setting up the drilled posts and marking the position of the thread hole in the mirror frame.

Then work out the required length with everything set up.

Posts, feet

The joint between the post and feet is optional, dowelled, tenoned or loose tongue all being suitable. These joints can be cut more easily while all the sections are still square – before any shaping takes place on the posts.

While the feet of the posts can again either be dowelled, tenoned or loose tongued, I would suggest that a loose tongue might actually be the best option: firstly, because to cut a tenon on a small piece like the foot could be quite tricky; secondly, dowelling is a little suspect partly because the amount of end-grain around the dowel means adhesion is not very good; also, the carcass does not provide much depth to play with.

A loose tongue provides a better gluing area than a dowel. At this stage rout the small housings in the carcass top to take this joint, using a hand-held router with a straight-edge clamped to both sides of the base; alternatively, use a couple of wooden sash bars and heads.

Pivot mechanism

It is also much easier to drill and set up the pivot mechanism for the tilt of the mirror while everything is still square. This action avoids having to make angled blocks in order to drill holes that need to be at 90°.

> "It is much easier to drill and set up the pivot mechanism for the tilt of the mirror while everything is still square"

Set up the drilled posts with the feet and clamp to the carcass. Using an offcut from the feet, or something that is of the same thickness, as a spacer block, place the block on the carcass, stand the mirror frame on it and clamp the frame to the posts.

Mark with a bradawl the position of the hole for the pivot thread and carefully drill. Cut the thread to length and glue in with epoxy resin.

Shaping

I made up some templates from the original full-size drawing, glued them to some MDF and cut them out.

The posts and both sets of feet can be cut out on a bandsaw and cleaned up by hand using spokeshaves and files. For those versed in template routing a bearing-guided router bit can be used.

The chamfers running round the edges of the posts are cut with convex and straight spokeshaves.

The chamfers on the post feet are all cut by hand using a ⅜in chisel with the bevel face down and carefully paring a neat return. The straight runs are so small that they can be pared as well.

The slope is carefully planed and the rounding cut with a chisel and finished with files and abrasive paper. These small pieces are difficult to hold in a conventional vice and just too low to be comfortable.

An engineering vice, with soft jaws fitted, is extremely handy for this sort of work, presenting it in a much more versatile position.

LEFT: Marking out the posts and feet from templates

BELOW: Post and foot detail

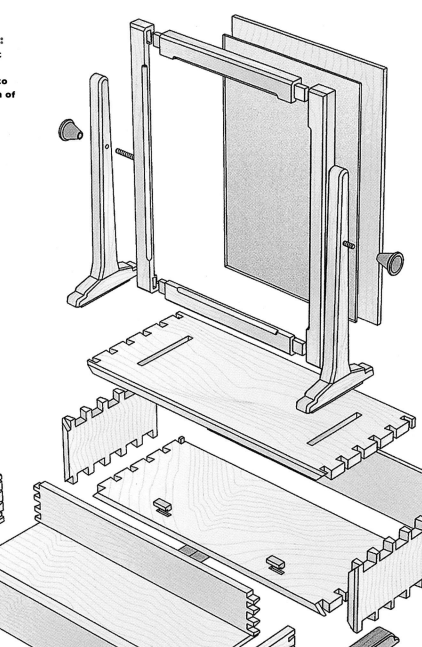

Abrasive paper glued down to 6mm MDF and cut with a bandsaw into various sized strips is useful for this type of hand-shaping – but the bandsaw will become very blunt! Using a series of different grades of paper provides a set of mini 'files' that are very good for getting into fiddly corners and places.

Carcass feet, backs

These were made the same way as the posts and feet, by using a template. They are screwed to the underside in line with the inside edge of the pin sockets. The backs are screwed into the rebates using No. 4⅝in brass screws.

Finish with several coats of Danish oil, cutting back in between every other coat, and glue and set up the posts and mirror. ■

MAQUETTES AND RODS

Every maker will have his or her own way of working. Some will work from the drawing board and have every last detail worked out, others will make maquettes and develop a piece as they go along.

Maquettes are especially useful when making something complicated like a chair for the first time. It can turn a two-dimensional drawing into a real life piece of furniture and show up problems – and solutions – that are not at all obvious on a drawing.

As they help potential clients to visualise their pieces, they are useful as marketing tools.

Another way of helping to work out the constructional details of a piece is to use a rod. I was taught to make a rod on a piece of board, a traditional method by which all dimensions are marked out against a straight edge of the board. All the joints are also marked with details of rebates etc. This rod is then used as a template, obviating, in theory at least, the need for a tape measure.

Using a rod helps me to work through the piece as I draw it out – like making it in two-dimensional form. It comes into its own when making more than one of something.

Cornering the

Mike Cowie makes a corner cupboard and tests his skills

● **MIKE COWIE
turned to
cabinetmaking
after being made
redundant 4 years
ago. He took a
City & Guilds
course at
Sheffield College
which he passed
with distinction,
set up his own
workshop, and is
now in the happy
position of
having as much
work as he can
cope with**

AT THE TIME I made this
corner cupboard, I wanted
to move away from the
rectilinear into more rounded
work, thus offering a broader
scope to potential clients. So, with
this in mind, I made a prototype,

in American cherry (*Prunus
serotina*) and white sycamore
(*Acer pseudoplatanus*), for
display purposes. It is a versatile
piece that could be used for
anything from a drinks' cabinet
to housing a TV or hi-fi.

Design

The design was an amalgam of
different ideas, not least of which was
a console table made by Alan Peters,
in rippled sycamore and maple.

The basic premise was to
establish a suitable arc, build a
frame around it, then joint up doors
to fit the gap – easily said! But it
was fun to do, and was certainly a
learning experience.

Despite the fact that it was
not a commission, it was
important that it was well
designed and made, because
I could not afford to waste
either the time or money on
an esoteric flight of fancy.

Carcass

The construction of the
carcass is fairly
straightforward – dovetailed
for strength and appearance
– I believe that hand-cut
dovetails are a pre-requisite
of bespoke furniture.

Door
construction

Some thought had to be
given to the construction
of the doors – although
they are simple enough in
theory. The arc is scribed
onto a piece of plywood
with the carcass
dimensions set out. This
is then divided into 25mm
(1in) segments, to be used
as a guide for the staves.
The arc is then bisected
and the resultant angle
retained on a sliding bevel.

Quartersawn timber is
used, cut into strips, 1050mm
(41⅜in) long, 30mm (1³⁄₁₆ in)
wide, and 25mm (1in) thick,
of which 26 pieces are
required, with possibly a
couple for spares. The finished
size is 25 by 22mm (1 by ⅞in)
– allowance being made to
flatten after cutting the staves, in
case of any stresses within the
wood. Prior to cutting, the grain
direction is marked on the top of
the boards, enabling similar
orientation for the doors.

**RIGHT: Alan
Peter's work
inspired the
curved and fluted
doors on this
piece**

market

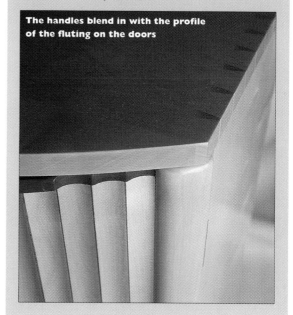

The handles blend in with the profile of the fluting on the doors

After planing and thicknessing to size, the pieces are graded and a large V is made to indicate position. Using the sliding bevel, with the angle taken earlier, the planer fence is adjusted to this angle and some test cuts done to establish accuracy. It would be possible to saw the staves directly from the solid to the indicated angle, but I elected for the planer and an equal amount of passes on each stave to the required dimensions.

Veneering

The staves are then placed on the plywood template and adjusted until they conform to the arc. Strips of American cherry veneer are cut the length of the staves, and glued and clamped to each side of each stave, except the side and centre outside pieces. When dry, the veneer edge is trimmed back with a sharp block plane – the end result being 26 Isosceles trapeziums, according to my daughter Claire!

ABOVE LEFT: The interior, with a solid American cherry back

Fine pinned dovetails and door-style detail

Drawer front and plinth are laminated around a plywood former

DIFFERENT APPROACHES

James Krenov in his book *The Fine Art of Cabinet Making* describes the alternative method of preparing and cramping curved doors. Krenov likes to hand-plane his joints and glue in stages, usually three, which, with a six stave door, would be three operations – two halves and then the middle joint. As he says, you have to be careful, particularly on the final glue-up as there is a tendency for the last pieces to spring because, at this stage, you have the greatest amount of curvature. He suggests using cramps on either side of the curve, one below and one above. The outside cramps can rest directly on the outside face of the joint which will give some downward pressure and help to stop it springing. A neat tip is to have a lamp or a torch handy to check both sides of the joint – they need to be spot-on, sawing apart a coopered door would not be fun!

Another approach to gluing up all the components of a door simultaneously is to use a jig, *see drawing*, although you may find that you have to use thin packing pieces to increase the pressure on the bottom of each edge – when it is an outer face it is important to get the joint right.

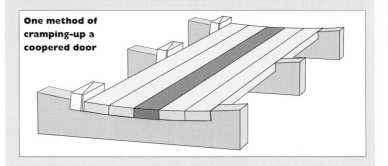

One method of cramping-up a coopered door

Coopering doors

The answer I found to gluing-up the doors is a method that has become a favourite – it is to use a spline running the length of the staves, thereby achieving an excellent reference without any side slip when pressure is applied. A 6mm (¼in) groove is cut on the spindle moulder, an inverted router, or even a tablesaw with adequate guarding. They are cut for a snug fit – neither too tight or too loose.

Next, the coved sections are cut on the spindle, using a rounded cutter, with test cuts being taken until a suitable shape emerges. Then a tunnel is formed with the guards, with which to pass the staves through safely. Both front and backs are coved in order to improve the look of the doors when open.

From my limited experience of coopered work, I have found that gluing-up in small sections promotes

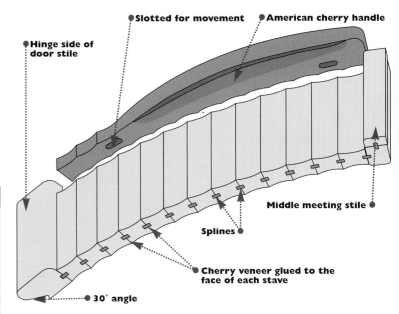

Hinge side of door stile

Slotted for movement

American cherry handle

Middle meeting stile

Splines

Cherry veneer glued to the face of each stave

30° angle

BISECTING AN ARC

1. Draw an arc, full size, enabling actual staves to be positioned on the template for accuracy, taking off more or less as required.
2. Divide into equal segments.
3. Bisect one of these divisions AC.
4. Draw a tangent to AB.
5. Take largest resultant angle to set planer fence – 93° Being part of a circle, all the staves will be at this angle.

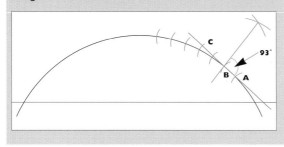

errors, and in this particular job there are no allowances – so to save wasting time, effort, and materials, each door is glued-up in one operation, which is a little tricky – although, with the aid of an 18mm (¹¹⁄₁₆in) plywood former, both top and bottom creating a sandwich, slow-setting glue such as Cascamite, space to work, and plenty of clamps, it's easy!

The same formers were used for both doors thereby ensuring

uniformity.

When I was in the process of making this piece, the coves unfortunately suffered a degree of splintering from the moulder cutters, and had a slight variance in the depth of cut – this was remedied by a scraper, shaped to fit, and a couple of hours hard work – oh for an apprentice! The result was a beautiful smooth surface from the hard sycamore.

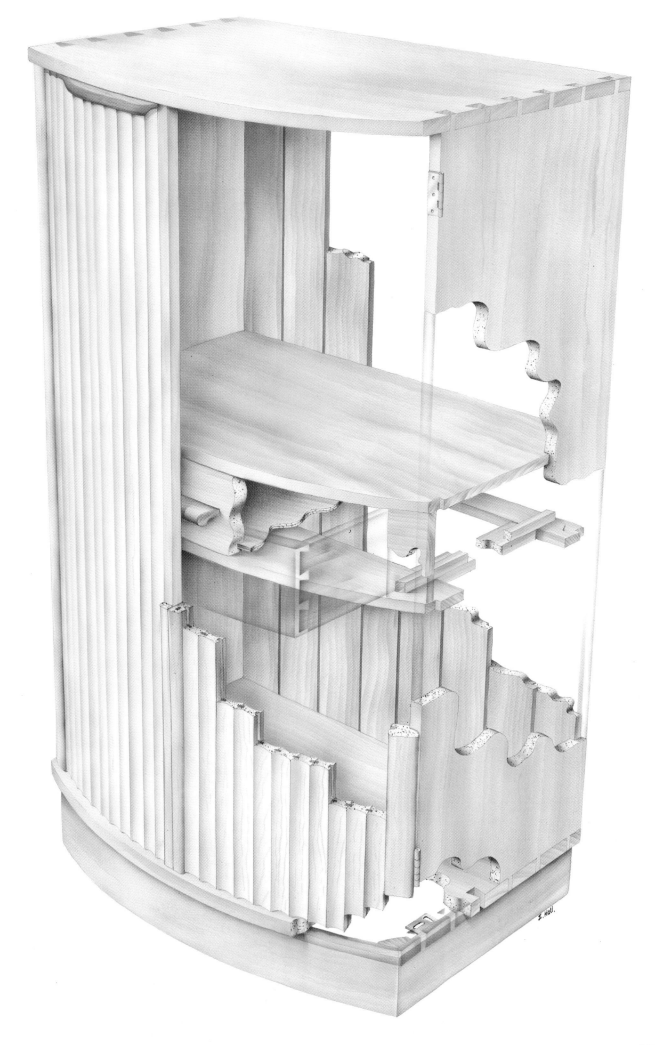

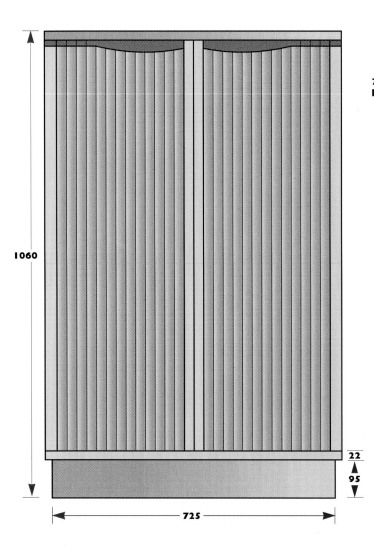

1060

22

95

725

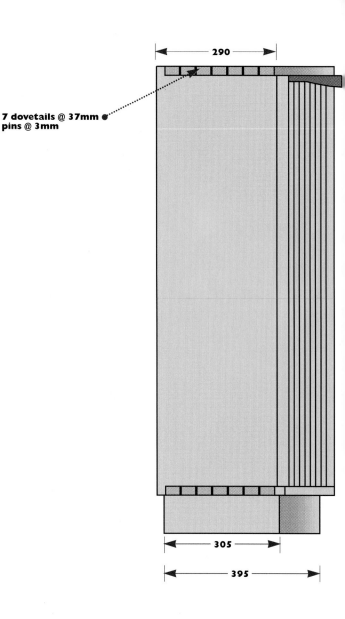

290

7 dovetails @ 37mm
pins @ 3mm

305

395

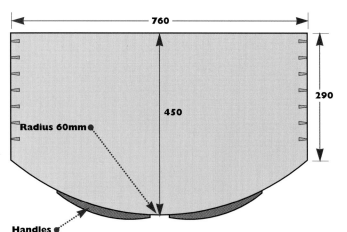

760

450

290

Radius 60mm

**Handles
protrude**

Fitting doors

Fitting the doors to the carcass presented a slight problem, solved by the gradual evolution of the door stiles as illustrated. The central section was arrived at similarly, which also has the advantage of covering any movement that inevitably will occur.

Plinth and drawer

The curved section of the plinth and drawer front are of similar construction – 3mm (⅛in) sawn veneer, glued round a plywood former. This method needs some care in cutting the dovetails.

The plinth is attached to the carcass with corner blocks and screws, through slots to allow movement. A central drawer is added – but, with hindsight, I would have used thinner bearer rails.

Finishing

All surfaces, particularly the coves, are sanded through the range of grits ending with 400, given a coat of sanding sealer, which is then finished with white polish, keeping it as white as possible. ◼

INSPIRATION

For inspiration, try viewing *Dovetail a drawer with Frank Klousz* by Taunton Videos – it was a turning point for me! Price: £16.95
Available from: GMC Publications Ltd, 166 High Street, Lewes, East Sussex BN7 1XU Tel: 01273 488005
Fax: 01273 478606

REFERENCE

The Fine Art of Cabinet Making by James Krenov published by Sterling
ISBN 0 8069 8572 0
Available through GMC Publications Ltd, 166 High Street, Lewes, East Sussex BN7 1XU
Tel 01273 488005 Fax 01273 478606

A table of substance

Brendan Devitt-Spooner makes a rosewood dining table

THE INSPIRATION for this dining table came when I was lucky enough to buy a large quantity of Borneo rosewood (*Melanorrhoea curtisii*). With 35 cube of it tucked up in an already overcrowded workshop, and an exhibition on the horizon, I decided to use some of the part-machined planks for the top of a dining table. At this stage I was still in the dark as to the timber's workability and finished appearance!

Design
Until someone comes up with the ultimate table design, that needs no legs or underframe to interfere with sitters' legs, a table must have supports. This can range from a single pedestal with radiating legs, through the standard four legs at the corners, to the highly extravagant lifelike forms of John Makepeace. But, whatever structure is chosen, the main function must be the support of the top. It would seem rather pretentious to design an underframe that looked fabulous, but was incapable of supporting six pairs of elbows.

My design was based around the triple tenon joint that links the two ends by a single rail.

Size
The first stage in making this table is to start with the top. Five of my planks measured 2743 by 203 by 50mm (108 by 8 by 2in) and had already been part machined.

Bearing in mind that to sell a dining table off the exhibition stand, a sensible size is deemed necessary, I decided to make it 2133mm (7ft). This also helped with the physical problem of moving the table around – at about 65lb a cube it is no lightweight!

Top
After re-machining a face side and face edge, and then thicknessing to 45mm (1¾in), the boards are then shot by hand for gluing together. Sometimes the surfacer plays ball and you end up with edges that need no further attention – but not always!

I do not rely on glued edges, and always use birch ply loose tongues. Using an old 6mm (¼in) slotting cutter on a spindle, I find the birch ply is a much tighter fit.

Twin stopped grooves are worked on each edge stopping at 25mm (1in) from each end. Before going ahead with this process, it is wise to mark out the end curves so that you can plot the groove ends.

● **BRENDAN DEVITT-SPOONER is a former teacher who turned to furniture-making and design in 1987. Largely self-taught, he takes a delight in using solid wood and has a preference for English timber**

RIGHT: A modern variation on a traditional theme – the trestle table taken a stage further

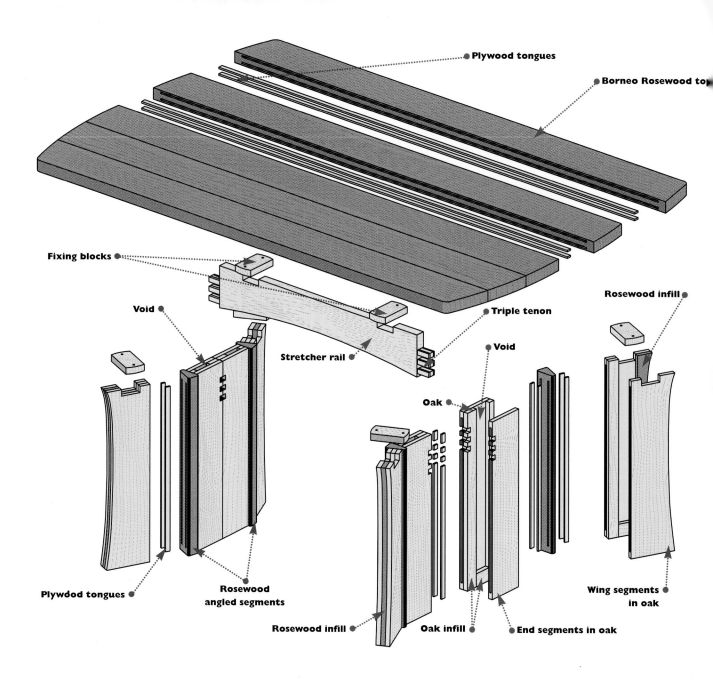

Plywood tongues

Borneo Rosewood to[p]

Fixing blocks

Void

Triple tenon

Rosewood infill

Stretcher rail

Void

Oak

Plywdod tongues

Rosewood
angled segments

Rosewood infill

Oak infill

End segments in oak

Wing segments
in oak

Ply tongues

With all the grooving done, the next stage is to prepare the ply tongues. Because it is such a tight fit, I reduce the thickness of the ply slightly, until it is a push fit. When the glue is applied, the ply and timber will swell ever so slightly – enough to prevent a calm assembly.

Because of the length of the grooves and gluing surfaces, it is best to only glue-up two planks at a time, which prevents the glue from beginning to set and makes it easier to manhandle.

The gluing boards are placed in a row of T-bar cramps – don't forget to protect the timber and cramp faces by placing paper between them.

When you come to glue-up the next stage, check the edges are still true. The cramping forces may have altered it and it will need to be attended to – this is where it starts getting heavy!

"Getting the fit right is important – it is one place the client will look at and judge your work by"

Final surface

In a couple of days time you will have a large top that needs planing, scraping and sanding. Unless you know a friendly firm that has a thicknessing sander, the next two to three days will seem very long.

With quite a twisted grain in places, I found my trusty Record No 80 scraper invaluable. The sanding process needs no elaboration. When you think it is finished, lightly damp the surface, which highlights any undetected scratches that can then be removed before the finish is applied.

At this stage I like to leave the top for a while. If you are worried that it may cup slightly whilst unrestrained, screw two substantial bearers to the underneath, where the frame will eventually sit. If these bearers are made longer than the width of the top, it helps protect the top if it is leant up against a wall.

Underframe

The design of the underframe was based on previous tables that I have made – the major difference being that I did not have any 50mm (2in) oak, but I did have a lot of 25mm (1in), so rather than glue two 25mm (1in) boards together, to achieve the required thickness, I decided to sandwich a piece of rosewood in between them, *see drawing*.

The oak is machined up at 19mm (¾in) thick, and sawn to 177mm (7in) widths for the wings, and 159mm (6¼in) widths for the ends. These ends

are loose tongued. When dry, the whole lot is thicknessed again, down to 27mm (1¹⁄₁₆in).

The infill pieces, the rosewood for the outsides and oak for the insides, are thicknessed to 19mm (¾in) and, using a vast number of G cramps, the six laminated sections are glued-up. Because the final dimensions are based on the outside parts of the sandwich, leave the infill pieces protruding slightly. Then, when dry, they can be planed to size.

Wings

The curve on the outside of the wings is a matter of taste. It is a good idea to mark all four wings with a French curve, and then position them in the final form to ensure that the grain directions look flowing. Using a bandsaw to remove the waste, keep the waste parts for pressure pads when gluing.

The vertical posts between the laminated sections are cut from 75 by 50mm (3 by 2in) pieces of rosewood. After initial surfacing and thicknessing, the angled faces are made by canting over the table sawblade to 12.5° and passing each piece in both directions, keeping the wider base part up against the fence. The angled faces are then surfaced and put aside, ready for grooving.

Grooving

All the posts and sandwiches are then grooved for loose tongues. Apart from making a strong joint, it also helps for

alignment when gluing. Using a few short pieces of ply, the ends can be dry assembled to see how they look.

Main joint

Before gluing, the main joint has to be tackled, which is, essentially, quite straightforward. The real concerns are accuracy in marking and cutting.

Remove most of the waste from the mortices by drilling it out on a pillar drill, and then cutting to the line using a chisel. Don't forget that the outside face mortice will be slightly wider than the inside, to make space for the wedges.

The tenon cheeks are cut on a bandsaw and the remaining parts are done by hand. It is a good idea to make the tenons longer than needed. A small chamfer is worked around each end of each tenon which makes entry easier and also prevents the tenon from creating any breakout in the mortice. Getting the fit right is important – it is one place the client will look at and judge your work by.

With all the joint work done, the long curve on the main rail can be sawn and cleaned up. A 13mm (½in) radius is formed along the curves, using a router and a bearing guided cutter.

Assembly

With all the major work done on the underframe, it can now be sanded and finished. Using a pad sander, work from 100 grit to 240 grit and then finish with two coats of Danish oil.

The two ends and main rail can now be glued together. Have the appropriate wedges already prepared and, with the joints held tight with sash cramps, carefully drive in the wedges. Note that the force exerted by the wedge is across the grain. Hit them in too much and you will end up with

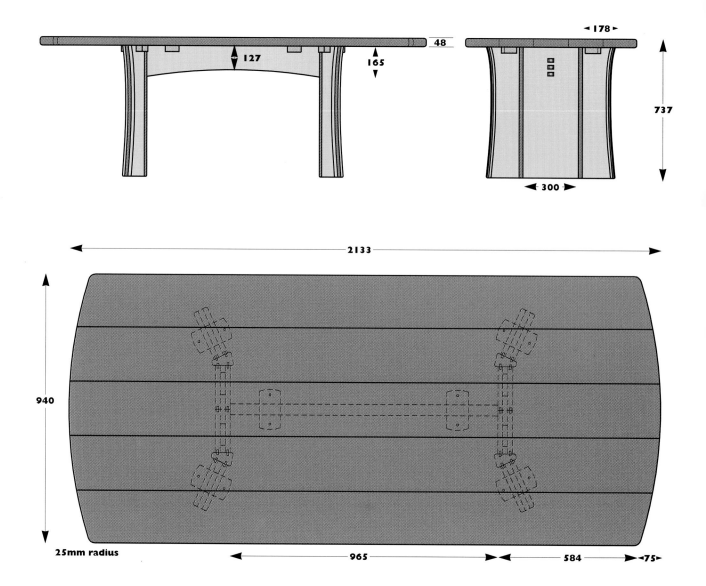

a split that wasn't intended! Knock them in with a hammer until the gaps have all closed up, and then just a little more.

Final glue-up

Whilst this assembly is drying, the curves on the wings can be cleaned up using a spokeshave, and the radii formed using the router. The radii on the posts also need to be formed. Because the corners are not 90°, these can be done by hand using a plane, and then sanded. Be careful not to sand into the joint surface.

The final glue-up is probably the hardest in that you do not have many 90° corners to pull up. I find that it is easier to glue the posts to the wings first, using the waste from the curve, suitably padded to aid a uniform pressure.

When dry, the wing assemblies can be glued to the main frame. With careful positioning of the cramps, and lots of softwood blocks, it should not cause too many anxious moments.

Last stages

The last stages in completing the underframe lie with filling the voids on the bottom with appropriate pieces of

oak, and then cleaning up the bottom surface. This is necessary as it allows the table to slide on carpet.

A radius is worked around the bottom to prevent a ragged edge being formed. After spending a lot of time sanding the bottom, protect this surface from scratching by placing on an old piece of carpet.

The sections have to be cut out to accommodate the blocks which hold down the top. Because the void in the wings was 75mm (3in) wide, I made all the blocks this width and cut out 25.4mm (1in) deep sections on the four wings, and at each end of the main frame – these are then levelled using a straight cutter in a router.

Because the frame and the top will move the same way when subjected to varying humidities, these blocks can be screwed directly to the underframe, and have holes rather than slots for screwing into the top.

Back to the top

With the underframe completed, attention can now return to the top. Firstly the ends need to be shaped. Mark out the curve required and prepare to cut. Because of the weight of the top, it is a good idea to leave the

table top where it is and use a jigsaw, if you have one – alternatively you can use a bandsaw. Unfortunately I didn't have a jigsaw, but with the judicious use of lots of people and odd roller stands I managed to rough a fair curve.

With a template of the curve in plywood cramped to the end, the edge is cleaned up, using a bearing guided straight cutter. The ends are sanded, starting with 80 grit and finishing with 240 grit. The radii on the edges are then formed, using a 13mm (½in) bearing cutter set at less than full depth, in order to give a definite line around the edge.

Before attaching the top to the underframe, the underside of the top is given two coats of Danish oil. The top is held down with 38mm (1½in) no.12 brass countersunk screws. The top is oil finished.

Conclusion

I was impressed with this psuedo rosewood – the colour is rich and it worked well, even though it was hard and quite abrasive. The only downside is that most people at exhibitions seem to prefer lighter colour timbers for dining tables, so I have still got one extremely heavy Borneo rosewood dining table for sale! ■

Weight of history

ADDITIONAL PHOTOGRAPHY BY CHRIS SKARBON

John Lloyd on the heavy side of traditional furniture-making

THE MOST COMMON type of early dining table, often listed in 15th century inventories, was of trestle construction. In these, large boards of oak (*Quercus sp.*) or elm (*Ulmus procera*) form a detachable top which rested on a number of supports.

These tables were often removed after meals, which is of course the perfect end to a perfect meal - manhandling a huge slab of oak must be a wonderful aid to digestion!

The other form of dining table around in the 15th century was the 'joyned' table, which consisted of – usually turned – legs which were 'joyned' by means of rails and stretchers with mortice and tenon joints.

These were also of very heavy construction and had the benefit, if you were a diner, in that they were not of 'knock-down' construction; however, the huge bulbous legs that were popular from the late 16th-century meant that you certainly knew about it if you got the leg!

My design brief for this project was for the trestle form of table which was made in the early 16th century; it was to have curved supports at each end linked by rails at the top and a single stretcher passing through the uprights and secured by wedges.

The size of the top was also prescribed, dictated by the size of the room and the number of people required to be seated around the table.

French connection

The wood decided upon was oak, at my suggestion of the quarter-sawn brown variety.

The construction of the table in terms of joints and so on was, therefore, going to be fairly straightforward; the challenge turned out to be in sourcing the oak and its subsequent handling while converting and jointing.

My first lead for the timber was a local estate which had, apparently, two butts of brown oak tucked away.

When I arranged to inspect them it was found that they had mysteriously vanished – it was suggested that an estate worker may have cut them up for fence posts because the wood was a funny colour!

Luckily the French have a much less haphazard approach to the management of their forests; it seems that their standing trees are listed, and if an oak tree is brown oak it is recorded as such.

Consequently the wood was imported from France, and an afternoon was spent sifting through several butts of brown oak – no mean feat when the boards you are sifting are over 50mm (2in) thick, 480mm (19in) wide and 4 metres (12ft) long! Having picked the butt with the best figure and most even colour it was transported to a local sawmill, to be converted into slightly more manageable pieces.

ABOVE: Plenty of French brown oak

BELOW: End cleats are loose-tenoned into stopped grooves

"It was suggested that an estate worker may have cut the brown oak up for fence posts because the wood was a funny colour!"

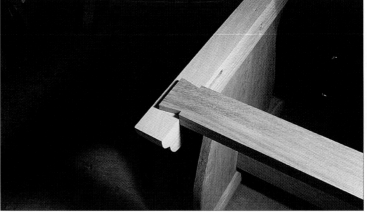

"To keep stress levels to a minimum I like to have as much as possible under my control when gluing up"

Table top

The boards selected for the table's top are from the centre of the butt – these have the best figuring – and to give a symmetrical appearance each was split into two 25mm (1in)

boards and arranged in three pairs around the centre line of the top.

Having planed and thicknessed the boards there is just the small question of jointing them. I do not possess a planer with tables the length of Brighton Pier so this meant resorting to my trusty No. 8 jointer, and a great deal of heaving big lumps of wood around.

Balancing these huge boards on their mating edges and, with a light source behind, peering along the join to find the high spots was

followed by more heaving, a bit of judicious planing, yet more heaving and peering until the perfect joint was attained!

To keep stress levels to a minimum I like to have as much as possible under my control when gluing up. To this end, five dowels or biscuits were used in each joint to keep the top surfaces in register and the boards glued up in pairs, taking care to protect the freshly-planed edges from indentations from the cramps.

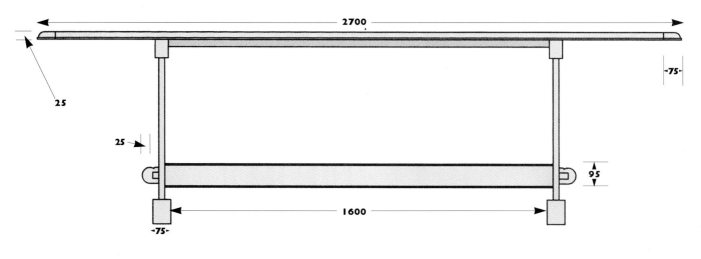

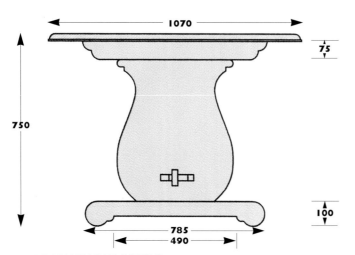

"Because of the length of the stretcher and the rather confined space in my machine shop, I cut the shoulders of the tenons by hand"

Biscuit jointed top

End cleat

Loose tongue

Buttons

Bearer

Triple mortice and tenon

Rails with dovetail joints

Foot

Stretcher rail with loose wedged tenon

> "Manhandling a huge slab of oak must be a wonderful aid to digestion!"

Once the top was in one piece it was checked and trimmed to its final finished size. The cleats are fitted to the ends of the table with loose tongues – a router with a bearing-guided cutter was used to cut stopped grooves in the cleats and table ends for these.

Trestle ends
The shaped trestle ends are made up in width by jointing boards symmetrically as with the table's top.

These are then jointed to the top bearers and feet with mortices and tenons – the tenons are triple to counteract shrinkage. The shaping of the trestles is the only area which

requires any design input and this is just a question of drawing and re-drawing the curves full size until they look right.

Before gluing up the trestles various joints must be cut into the top bearers for the rails and securing the top. The two rails are jointed to the top bearers with single lapped dovetails.

BELOW LEFT:
Stretcher must be pulled up tight...

BELOW RIGHT: ... by wedged key – make sure the key projects evenly each side of the tenon

ABOVE: Pocket screw, centre, and buttons fix the top to the base, allowing movement while keeping the top centred

"Finally use one of those razor-sharp chisels to trim back to the scribed lines"

The bulk of the waste from the socket may be removed with a router, but it is a good idea to make an angled saw cut just inside the scribed lines at each end of the socket before switching the router on.

Finally use one of those razor-sharp chisels to trim back to the scribed lines, and a skew chisel to clean up the internal corners.

The fixing of the top is achieved using a pocket-screw at the centre and shrinkage buttons at either end of the bearers. This arrangement will allow movement of the top whilst keeping the top centrally on the bearers. These pockets and the grooves for the buttons are also cut before gluing up.

Finishing off

The final element of the table is the stretcher rail, which has a through keyed tenon at either end. Because of the length of the stretcher and the rather confined space in my machine shop, I cut the shoulders of the tenons by hand with the tenons themselves being cut on the bandsaw.

Sockets must be cut in the tenons for their wedged keys – these should extend a little way behind the face of the trestles to allow the wedges to pull the joints up nice and tight.

Lastly, make two wedges. This sounds very simple but as with most aspects of making, it is a good idea to do a full size drawing before attacking an innocent piece of wood. In this case, draw a plan view of the end of the stretcher showing the socket for the wedge, then draw in a wedged key that will fit through the sockets with an even amount protruding at each end. Once satisfied make a template and attack some wood.

Having sanded the whole table, raised the grain and sanded again, it was finished using several coats of shellac sanding sealer which was cut back with 0000 wire wool before being waxed with a hard, home-made wax.

Colouring is, of course, completely unnecessary because of the wonderful natural colour of the timber – which is the reason brown oak was selected in the first place. ■

JOHN LLOYD turned to restoration from project management when he found himself spending more time in front of a computer than on the building site. He trained with Bruce Luckhurst and gained a City & Guilds silver medal in Furniture Advanced Crafts. After sharing workshops at Bow and Battersea he struck out on his own, moving to Bolney, West Sussex three years ago where he restores and copies mainly traditional furniture for a largely private client base. He has also restored for Sotheby's, Christies and the National Trust.

Mark out and cut the dovetails at the ends of the rails and, using these as templates, scribe the dovetails onto the bearers – being sure to mark which one goes where – and extend the lines down the vertical face with a square, the thickness of the rail is transferred using a cutting gauge.

LOW TECH MOULDING

To soften the top edges of the stretcher a bead is run along its length. This could be done with a router but I prefer, where possible, to go low tech and use a steel slotted woodscrew which has been inserted into a piece of beech.

The screw's head then becomes a cutting edge, so has its face sharpened on an oil stone. The width of the bead produced by this tool is governed by how far the screw projects from the piece of wood which acts as the fence, but this isn't infinitely variable as the screw head must be angled so that the slot does the actual cutting.

To obtain a crisp edge to the bead set it in with a cutting gauge before starting work with the screw cutter, and if necessary finish shaping with a shoulder plane.

Another low tech approach to mouldings is the scratchstock, which has been around since medieval times. This is another easy way to make simple mouldings of a greater variety, limited only by the shapes you can invent, file and grind.

In some instances the scratchstock can be as quick as a router, particularly for a small run of a one-off moulding on a curve – by the time you've made a jig for the router, a scratchstock can be made out of an old piece of bandsaw or hacksaw blade and a piece of scrap wood. It is certainly cheaper than buying special router cutters.

If you want to make an especially smart scratchstock refer to Bob Wearing's book, *Hand Tools for Woodworkers*, ISBN 0 7134 7223 5, published by Batsford at £15.99.

ABOVE: Low tech moulding device – an offcut and a woodscrew
BELOW: Cutting a bead with the screw's slot

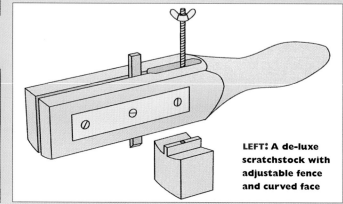

LEFT: A de-luxe scratchstock with adjustable fence and curved face

Taking a bow

PHOTOGRAPHY BY STEPHEN HEPWORTH, MAIN
ILLUSTRATION BY IAN HALL

● **ANDREW LAWTON**, a member of the Society of Designer Craftsmen, has been making furniture full time since 1980. He rescued Goatscliffe Workshops – run by pioneer craftsman Ben Coopland from the 1920s to the 1960s in Grindleford, Derbyshire – from near dereliction. Lawton's 1991 Spiral Table in English walnut inlaid with sycamore received a Guild Mark from the Worshipful Company of Furniture Makers.

ABOVE: Photo 1 An alternative to the frame and panel back – solid with skewed dovetails

MANY TRADITIONAL corner cupboards suffer from the same weakness: the carcasses, particularly the backs, are often of a lower standard of craftsmanship than the doors and leading edges.

Antique examples usually have nailed-on pine backs while modern reproductions invariably sport a thin ply panel, at best screwed, at worst stapled on.

Andrew Lawton makes a bow-fronted corner cabinet

We can do much better than that. A sound job should be properly framed up and panelled, if solid timber is being used, or where a flush interior is called for, the carcass can be assembled from lipped, veneered MDF or other manufactured board.

A third method, which lends itself particularly well to relatively small, wall-mounted pieces is a solid timber carcass jointed with skewed dovetails, *see photo 1*. The cabinet described here is just such a piece, the latest of many similar and related cabinets I have made over the past eighteen years, *see photo 2*.

55

Planning

Despite its apparent simplicity, this is an exacting piece to make and has to be tackled in the right order, beginning with a full drawing of the doors as if they were flat, not curved, accurate templates of the carcass, top and bottom, and doors.

In cabinetmaking, the doors can be, and usually are, made after the carcass has been put together, but here they must be made first to ensure that the faceting of the doors accurately follows the stepped edges of the carcass, which is a salient feature of the design.

If, after gluing up, it is found that the doors don't quite match the templates, being either a little too sharply or gently curved, the top and bottom can be made to match, and the eye will never notice.

Doors

The doors of this piece are not simply sets of tapered slats of solid timber shot to an angle and glued-up as in classic coopered fashion. It is possible, and easier, to make them that way, but it is an extra risk. There is always the chance that long-term changes in relative humidity could cause the doors to go out of shape.

Method

The method used here is to sandwich lengths of MDF between two skins of thick, bandsawn veneer. The veneers have to be fairly thick to allow the segments to step back and forwards alternately, see fig 1.

The thin segments are faced with 3.5mm (⅛in) veneers and the thick slats with 6mm (¼in). On no account should veneers of different thicknesses be mixed on the same slat since this could cause an unequal pull, and consequent distortion.

Prior to veneering, the slats should be end-lipped, not to disguise the fact that they are MDF and to pass

them off as solid timber; but because raw MDF is not attractive. The doors of this cabinet are end-lipped with a deliberately darker coloured elm to emphasise the construction rather than conceal it – the client was made aware of this and why it was done.

The two outer slats of each door, the counterparts of the hinging and meeting stiles of a conventional door, are done slightly differently in that they are single-direction laminated, again for dimensional stability. Alternatively these segments could have a long edge-lipping applied before being veneered.

Veneers

The veneers were cut from several matching boards from the same tree, using the bandsaw, but could just as easily be done on a circular saw, although this would be more wasteful.

They are glued on with Cacamite, evenly applied with an old photographic roller.

All ten slats are faced at one go between eight sash-cramps with several thicknesses of MDF on the outsides to even out the pressure. A couple of sheets of newspaper are slipped between each slat to act as a cushion and prevent them from sticking together. It has to be admitted that this method is somewhat Heath Robinson compared to using a vacuum press, but in small spaces it can be a good alternative.

Dummy run

After cleaning up, the slats are sawn to the trapezoid shape taking measurements directly from the full size drawing, and the edges shot to the required angle on a surface planer with the fence tilted.

A dummy run should be carried out first using scrap to ensure that the angles conform to the door templates.

ABOVE: Photo 2 Wych elm and tapered panels provide an interesting angle on corner cupboards

In the absence of a machine planer the joints could be shot by hand with a try plane, using a sliding bevel with an angled jig to help maintain a consistent angle. A jig of this description is used to guide the router when machining the grooves in each abutting joint, into which a ply tongue is fitted when assembling the doors, *see photo 3*.

Door assembly

Each door is assembled dry, complete with ply tongues, to check that all the butt joints will pull up tightly.

"Prior to veneering, the slats should be end-lipped, not to disguise the fact that they are MDF and to pass them off as solid timber, but because raw MDF is not attractive"

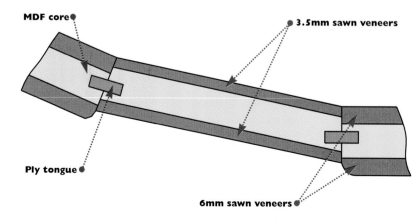

Fig 1. Section of door segments

MDF core

3.5mm sawn veneers

Ply tongue

6mm sawn veneers

TOP: Photo 3 An angled jig ensures plywood tongues are the correct angle to parallel joints in coopered door

ABOVE: Photo 4 Cramping the door up, G-cramps exert downward pressure to avoid springing

By using sash-cramps to squeeze the slats together, balanced by G-clamps at each end to exert downward pressure, it is possible to achieve tight joints. If necessary, a central sash-cramp may be needed, but you can't use a G-clamp here to pull downwards – a supply of weights will give the down-thrust.

A practise run with a door made of plain MDF or cheap timber is strongly recommended before risking spoiling the real thing.

Rather than gluing-up on the bench, the cramps are best rested on a pair of trestles to enable the joints to be inspected from underneath and any excess glue removed without having to manhandle the whole assembly, *see photo 4*.

After the glue has set, overnight if possible, the doors can be removed from the cramps and checked for twisting on a flat surface and against the templates; if all is well they can be put to one side and a start made on the carcass.

Carcass

The first step is to machine up enough timber for the top, the bottom, the two halves of the back, and as many shelves as required.

The back halves should be carefully trued-up to form perfect rectangles and then shot to conform to the template, *see photo 5*. Note that the angle of the apex of the back should be slightly more than 90°. This is to create a small area of clearance when the cabinet is attached to the wall and

CHOICE OF TIMBER

The choice of timber, irrespective of species, needs careful consideration for this design to be successful. Straight grained, preferably quarter-sawn material is best, for its dimensional stability and resistance to shrinkage, *see fig 3*.

This is good from an aesthetic angle too, since, because of its emphasis on vertical lines; a wild boisterous grain would fight with the faceting of the doors and look restless.

Client's choice

In this case the client had asked for wych elm (*ulmus glabra*), selected from my own stocks which were bought as round logs from the local authority, quarter sawn at a local mill and seasoned on our premises in the early 1980's.

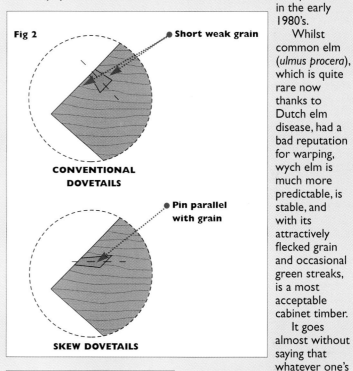

Whilst common elm (*ulmus procera*), which is quite rare now thanks to Dutch elm disease, had a bad reputation for warping, wych elm is much more predictable, is stable, and with its attractively flecked grain and occasional green streaks, is a most acceptable cabinet timber.

It goes almost without saying that whatever one's choice of wood, kiln dried or not, its moisture content must be around the 10% mark, or less, in order to stand up to the rigours of central heating.

LEFT: Although both carcass back and end can move together owing to the 45° orientation, ends tend to move more than the backs – hence quartersawn timber preferable

ensures that there will be no gaps at the front, since walls are rarely true either in old or modern houses.

Again using the template, the ends of the carcass are prepared, preferably together, and the shoulder-lines for the dovetails marked with a gauge.

The doors are now offered up to the ends and the exact outline drawn with a sharp pencil, followed by a 3 or 4mm (⅛ or ⁵⁄₃₂ in) allowance for the overhang of the carcass edges.

The steps on the leading edge are best cut with a router against a securely anchored straight edge, moved around the workpiece as each

facet is worked, followed by removal of the sharp corners.

The aim is to continue the slope of the faceting of the doors across the top and bottom of the carcass.

Dovetails

Conventional dovetails are not suitable for jointing this cabinet since the angle of the grain direction would result in short, and therefore weak, joints – quite apart from the aesthetic consideration, *see panel, fig 2*. Skewed, or bevelled dovetails are therefore the answer, set out with either a sliding bevel or purpose-made template.

The slope angle should be equidistant around a 45° centreline, with a pitch of 1 in 7 or 8 as in normal dovetails.

The tails are cut on the top and bottom with a dovetail saw, the bulk of the waste removed with a coping saw and the remainder gently pared back to the line with a chisel or chisels.

Getting right into the corner can be tricky – a fine 3mm (⅛in) bevel-edge chisel is very useful here.

Transfer to carcass

Once the tails are cut, the workpiece can be transferred to the carcass back, and the pins marked with a knife or scriber, ensuring that nothing slips out of alignment.

Cutting the pins is again done with the dovetail saw, coping saw, and chisel. A useful way of speeding up this operation is to use the router in conjunction with a simple but accurate L-shaped jig, set dead level with the top of the pins, instead of paring down to the shoulder line by hand.

These dovetails may look a little unfamiliar and daunting, but are not much more difficult than their more conventional relatives.

Securing the carcass back in the vice to prevent vibration while the joints are cut is usually the biggest headache.

If desired, though not essential, the corners of the carcass can be mitred in a similar way to Colin Eden-Eadon's toilet mirror, *see page 34*. This is an added refinement which does frame the doors rather nicely, *see photos 6 & 7*.

Gluing-up

Once the dovetails have been checked over and it is certain they will all locate and pull up to the shoulders, the carcass can be glued-up using sash-cramps and stout blocks to spread the pressure. Again, the assembly must be tested to ensure that it is out of wind before being left to set thoroughly.

After cleaning up the outside, the doors can be fitted, hinged and hung.

Door-pulls are a matter of choice.

On this cabinet simple handles, tapered to match the slope of the door facets, are worked from laburnum (*laburnum anagyroides*), which compliments the elm quite effectively. They are dovetailed onto the doors, giving extra interest as well as a secure fixing, *see photo 8*.

Shelves

The penultimate stage is the shaping and fixing of the two shelves. These

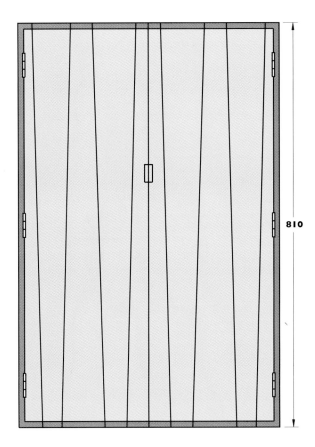

810

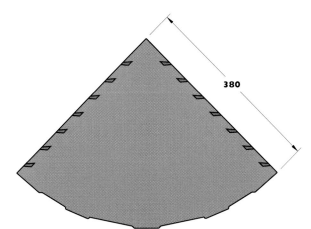

380

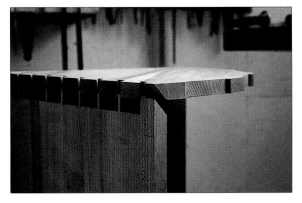

DOOR HANGING

Mark the vertical centre line of the cabinet on the inside faces of the top and bottom.

For each door in turn, shoot the hinging edge to fit, then the top and bottom edges until the door will just enter.

Then shoot the closing edge until it is a fraction proud of the centre line. Hinge both doors and hang. Remove a shaving or two top and bottom to allow clearance for the doors to open without binding on the carcass.

Finally, remove shavings from the closing edges until the doors just meet, and the adjacent facets are both in line with each other and parallel to the corresponding steps of the carcass.

If you get plane-happy and remove too much wood from the vertical edges when fitting, the doors can simply be set slightly further back into the body of the cabinet – something you can't do with an ill-fitting pair of doors in a parallel-sided cabinet!

Catches

When the doors are fitting snugly, catches of your choice can be fitted. I have often used miniature bullet-catches in the past, sinking the body of the catch into the carcass, dispensing with the striking plate and letting a section of dense hardwood, such as ebony, end-grain-on into the end of the door.

But increasingly I use 8mm (⁵⁄₁₆in) diameter magnetic catches, which are not so unobtrusive but have the advantage of an easily adjustable keeper-plate and, with no moving parts, an almost indefinite life.

are simple quadrants with bevelled edges, secured from the back with screws, the heads of which are counter-bored and pelleted.

This method of attachment is perfectly adequate since cabinets of this type are only ever likely to carry the weight of glasses and other light objects.

The shelves are left until last so that they don't get in the way when the doors are being hung.

Finish

Finally, the surface finish can be applied. Elm looks best in my opinion with a low lustre finish – this piece is treated with several thin coats of Danish oil to enhance the appearance and give a reasonable degree of surface protection.

Fixing

The completed cabinet can be fixed to the wall in a number of ways. In this instance, four counterbored holes were drilled just inside the doors, with removable plugs of elm covering the screw-heads, to facilitate the removal of the cabinet for redecoration or relocation.

Whatever method is adopted, it is important that the natural movement of the carcass, with day to day changes in humidity, is not restricted – nor must the cabinet be distorted in any way, which would throw the doors out of alignment. ■

Staple fare

Mike Cowie makes a traditional linenfold chest

● MIKE COWIE turned to cabinetmaking after being made redundant 4 years ago. He took a City & Guilds course at Sheffield College which he passed with distinction, set up his own workshop, and is now in the happy position of having as much work as he can cope with

WHAT WOULD at one time have been staple fare for cabinetmakers, appears now to be exceptional – the traditional linenfold chest. Having made one myself, I was surprised by the comments it received and the interest that was shown in the linenfolds – I only wish the rest of my work attracted such attention!

A piece of this nature presents good exercise in frame and panel construction plus an opportunity to develop your carving skills – it is fairly straightforward but requires care and attention to detail, that can only be good for future projects.

"It is feasible for a 213mm panel to move up to 6mm"

Construction

The construction of the chest is made up of frame and panel – the main requirement being a good fit, allowing for the movement that will occur. How much movement depends on the dryness of timber, the cut – either flat-sawn or quartered – and whether the chest is destined to be in a centrally heated room. It is feasible for a 213mm (8 ½ in) panel to move up to 6mm (¼in).

ABOVE: The side panels

Frame

I decided to use English oak (*Quercus robur*) – this should be dimensioned to 73mm (2⅞in) by 21mm (⅞in) for the frame, choosing the best pieces for the top and front – cut to size and morticed and tenoned. It helps to mark these with the aid of a rod to ensure accuracy, the muntins being left until last to obtain a spot-on measurement.

When all items are morticed and tenoned, do a test fit and if you are happy, then draw a pencil line on the areas to be grooved for the panels – disassemble, and cut a 5mm (³⁄₁₆in) groove – this way I usually get the grooves where they want to be!

For continuity, mitre the corners of the legs, which I feel is the easiest solution. I was tempted to use splines but opted for a simple glue-joint, as there is plenty of surface area – all held together by sellotape – which achieved an excellent result!

Top

The top is of slightly different construction having mitred bridle joints at the corners – this was decided on because of the high stress that is to be imposed on it. Luckily this joint does not show on the front aspect.

Care should be exercised in the

"How about chamfering the edges?" I thought – and so I started on the inside where the mistakes wouldn't show"

construction of the top with trial assembles to obtain the exact measurements.

Chamfered edges

Having got this far, and looking at the assembled carcass, I decided that something was missing – apart from the panels! "How about chamfering the edges?' I thought – and so I started on the inside where the mistakes wouldn't show, and progressed to the outside, until there were no edges left.

Panels

The panels are all cut from the same board ensuring a good match of grain and colour. Again, these are thicknessed to 21mm (⅞in) and cut to size with the first task being to cut a 22 by 12mm (⅞ by ½in) rebate on the front face and a 12 by 4mm (½ by ⁵⁄₃₂in) rebate on the rear, leaving a 5mm (³⁄₁₆in) lip.

GLUING-UP

Prior to gluing-up, the carcass is assembled in sections and belt-sanded flush with a used 120 grit belt, then finished with an orbital sander. The carcass is then glued-up, cutting off any glue deposits whilst still rubbery, as wiping off when wet can inhibit the finish, particularly with oil.

Don't forget to put the panels in when gluing-up – I did, twice! Use a sharp jack-plane to smooth off the top surface, and level with a block plane to take off the arris all round.

The whole piece is then oiled with Danish oil, giving it five to six coats and allowing 24 hours between each, rubbing down with a webrax pad between coats.

Fit the hinges, and you have an impressive linenfold panel chest and plenty of experience gained in the making!

The chisels used are a Henry Taylor 20mm No4, Henry Taylor 20mm No6, Henry Taylor 6mm No4, a straight edged skew and two smaller gouges that fit the curves of the folds.

ABOVE: After initial routing with a cove bit, a block plane and a gooseneck scraper are used to clean up

RIGHT: A rectangle is chopped out to form the flat before the inner fold – the waste is routed out

BELOW: The outline of the folds are drawn on the ends ready for marking out with the chisels

Linenfolds

Linenfolds are carved on all the panels, starting at the back – the rationale being that by the time I reached the front panels the carving would be looking good!

Two equally-spaced grooves, 7 by 4mm (%₂ by %₂in) are run into the panels with the aid of the tablesaw – this could, of course, be achieved with a router with multi-passes.

On the rebated edge draw a shape that satisfies the required curves – which is used as a marker to cut to. The method I used was a router set with a 19mm cove cutter, but it would be better with a fixed router – although it could be done freehand, with care, if necessary.

The first stage is to make a cut 7mm (%₂in) deep, either side of the centre line leaving a 2mm (%₂in) margin in the centre. A similar cut is run 5mm (³⁄₁₆in) from each edge. Then, using the same cutter set according to the drawn shape, adjust

and remove the excess waste.

Next is the simple job of smoothing off, using a block plane and gooseneck scraper. Sandpaper, through the grits from 120 to 240, is then used together with a rubber sanding block to finish the surface.

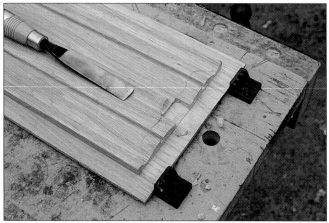

A gentle slope is carved on the ends and the small V-shape for the inner folds to be carved later

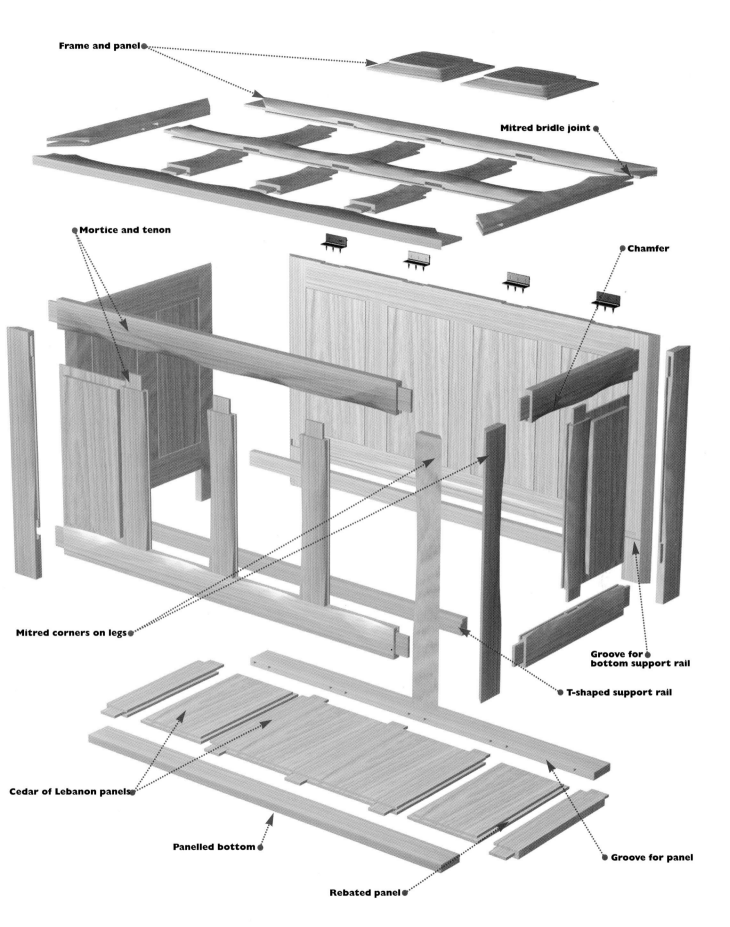

Frame and panel

Mitred bridle joint

Mortice and tenon

Chamfer

Mitred corners on legs

Groove for
bottom support rail

T-shaped support rail

Cedar of Lebanon panels

Panelled bottom

Groove for panel

Rebated panel

"Almost anything that conforms to the required radiuses will suffice –
hardly a purist approach but adequate!"

ABOVE: The previously drawn folds are now marked out with the appropriate chisels

TOP RIGHT: The folds marked out, ready for carving

ABOVE RIGHT: The first side is now complete

RIGHT: Under-cutting the middle folds

Outlines

The next task was one that I had to give some thought to and I decided that it would be best to work from the middle out.

With chisel in hand, chop a 20mm ($^{13}/_{16}$in) deep by 25mm (1in) rectangle, down to the level of the rebate – I think in future I would leave the odd 1 or 2mm ($^1/_{32}$ or $^1/_{16}$in) to finish later, as the greatest difficulty I found was that of over-cutting which telegraphs through. A small V is then cut out towards the edge, as indicated, which outlines the extent of the folds to be carved later.

Now remains the task of drawing an outline from which the folds can be carved. I thought that this would be the most difficult task and was pleasantly surprised to find that the folds guide the chisel – and the initial care taken is soon replaced by a more confident touch. Unsure which was the right chisel to use, and having a limited collection, I selected a Henry Taylor 20mm No 4, a 20mm No 6 and a 6mm No 4 – and managed to complete most of the work with them.

Starting from the marked outline, and holding the 20mm No 4 at an approximate angle of 30°, chop away the waste, leaving a 5mm ($^3/_{16}$in) edge and a nice bevel on which the folds can be drawn.

Ensure that all the curves are in the right place and preferably make light paring cuts, as oak can be a difficult timber to carve.

Folds

For the folds, first pencil in the outline then, using suitable chisels, make vertical cuts to conform to that outline, gradually paring away the waste until a satisfactory result is achieved. The primary tool I used was the 20mm No 6 followed by the 6mm No 4, and an assortment of indeterminate sizes, although anything that conforms to the required radiuses will suffice – hardly a purist approach but adequate! Especial care must be taken on the sharp curves as the wood is likely to splinter.

When finished, go over the outline with a sharp chisel and pare slightly to cut a clean smooth surface on the verticals, particularly the central section, trying to undercut slightly. A 6mm No 4 can then be used to bevel all the edges. Needless to say, the chisels should be as sharp as possible for all these tasks.

Finish

After a final check-over and a light sanding, it is time to apply a finish. As I mentioned earlier, the movement of the panels will, if finished in situ, lead to unsightly lines showing at the sides, so to avoid this, finish before gluing-up.

It was at this stage that I made my biggest error yet – I used garnet polish! I didn't like it, so off it had to come – and it was back to Danish oil, my favourite finish, which gives excellent results from a high gloss and satin, to matt, depending on the effort put in.

Fitting panels

For the fit of the panels allow 2mm ($^1/_{16}$in) on either side, allowing an 8 mm ($^5/_{16}$in) groove to be filled to 6mm ($^1/_4$in) but with a negligible gap at both the top and bottom so

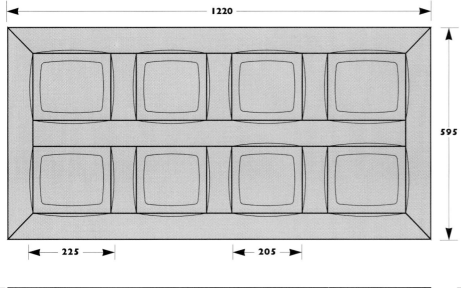

1220

595

225

205

"The method I used was a router set with a 19mm cove cutter, but it would be better with a fixed router – although it could be done freehand, with care, if necessary"

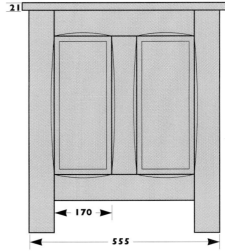

5

21

73

90

73

204

170

555

that it is a snug fit.

The top panels differ slightly from the lower, in shape, but also in that a normal fielded panel cutter was used. They didn't seem to fit quite right with the chamfering around the edges, so, taking the 6mm No 4 chisel that was used for the lower panels, I rounded off the corners and coved the edges, which gave a pleasing result.

For the bottom frame and panel construction I used oak with cedar of Lebanon (*Cedrus libani*) panels which give off a lovely aroma when you open the lid. These were set to the same dimensions as the sides, for continuity, and were fitted in place with the aid of a groove run in 25mm (1in) from the bottom of the frame, front and back – with a runner inserted into this, and the bottom sitting on it. ∎

The completed panel

SUPPLIERS

Suppliers of new carving chisels:
Henry Taylor (Tools) Ltd, Peacock Estate, Livesey St, Sheffield, S6 2BL
Tel 0114 234 0282 fax 0114 2852015
Ashley Iles (Edge Tools Ltd), East Kirkby, Spilsby, Lincolnshire, PE23 4DD
Tel 01790 763372 fax 01790 763610
For new and second-hand:
Bristol Design, 14 Perry Rd, Bristol, BS1 5BG
Tel 0117 929 1740

FURTHER READING

Essential Woodcarving Techniques by Dick Onians
GMC £15.95
ISBN 1 861108 042 5
Available from: GMC Publications Ltd, 166 High Street, Lewes, East Sussex BN7 1XU
Tel: 01273 488005 fax: 01273 478606

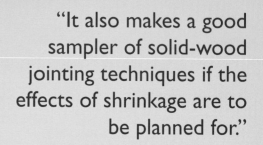

"It also makes a good
sampler of solid-wood
jointing techniques if the
effects of shrinkage are to
be planned for."

● GORDON DA'COSTA's visit to the Shaker Room at the American Museum in Bath was the furniture equivalent of conversion on the road to Damascus, and he took a City & Guilds course at Burnley, following this up with a licentiateship in Furniture and Manufacture. Passionate about Shaker furniture, he has yet to fulfil his ambition to visit the sites of now defunct communities in New England.

LEFT: Fall-front open to reveal interior layout

FAR LEFT: Fine Shaker style

Shaker-style desk

As well as being a useful piece of furniture, **Gordon da'Costa's** desk is an exercise in solid-wood joinery

THIS STYLE of desk offers practical storage for stationery and a good writing surface without looking too heavy, thanks to its open lower structure. It also makes a good sampler of solid-wood jointing techniques if the effects of shrinkage are to be planned for.

The base and top carcass are made separately. The base is a simple, table-like structure with rails tenoned into legs and fixed to the top carcass with buttons; the top is basically a box into which various sub-divisions and moving parts are fitted.

Using sliding dovetails for the corner joints of the outer carcass means that it will resist pushing forces in all directions, so although there's quite a lot going on inside, simple housing joints can be used for most internal fitting.

Wide components

The American cherry (*Prunus serotina*) I used measured 150 to 250mm (6 to 10in) in width, so the wider components were made up using loose tongues, where a groove is cut into both of the edges to be joined and a tongue of, say, cross-grain ply is inserted. Where end-grain is exposed, the grooves should stop 10mm ($^3/_8$in) or so short of the ends.

ABOVE: Sycamore drawer interior — dovetails and loper can also be seen

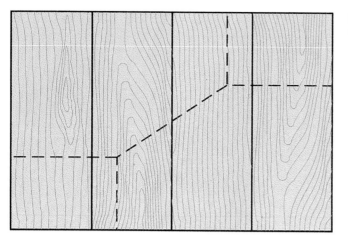

LEFT: Fig 1 Economic gluing — two carcass sides from one glue-up

BELOW: Fig 2 Alternative method of gluing up boards

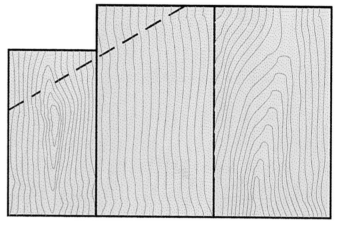

"A horizontal centreboard carries the fall-front's hinges and forms the back of the writing surface"

To minimise waste when making the sides, both can be glued up as a single 500mm by 820mm (19½ by 32in) piece, *see fig 1*, then cut as shown. Alternatively, use varying lengths, *see fig 2*.

RIGHT: Cherry and sycamore provide a pleasant contrast

Main carcass

The sides are jointed into the overhanging top and base using dovetailed housing joints. Dry assemble these to check the fit, then cut a rebate for the back.

On the inside face of the carcass top five housings for the drawer guides and pigeon holes are marked and cut. Housings are best cut with a router guided by a board clamped square across the work; it's a good idea to cut these before machining the parts that will fit into them so that the thickness can be matched to the cutter.

A horizontal centreboard carries the fall-front's hinges and forms the back of the writing surface. This is housed into the carcass sides; stop these housings 15mm (⅝in) short of the front edges and cut matching shoulders on the centreboard.

Two housings for the upper drawer guides are cut into this component to match those in the top carcass member, from which they should be marked.

Dry-assemble the base, top and sides of the carcass; slide in the centreboard and check for fit. When this is correct the edges of the top and bottom can be rounded and the sliding dovetails glued — but not the centreboard.

The illustration shows that

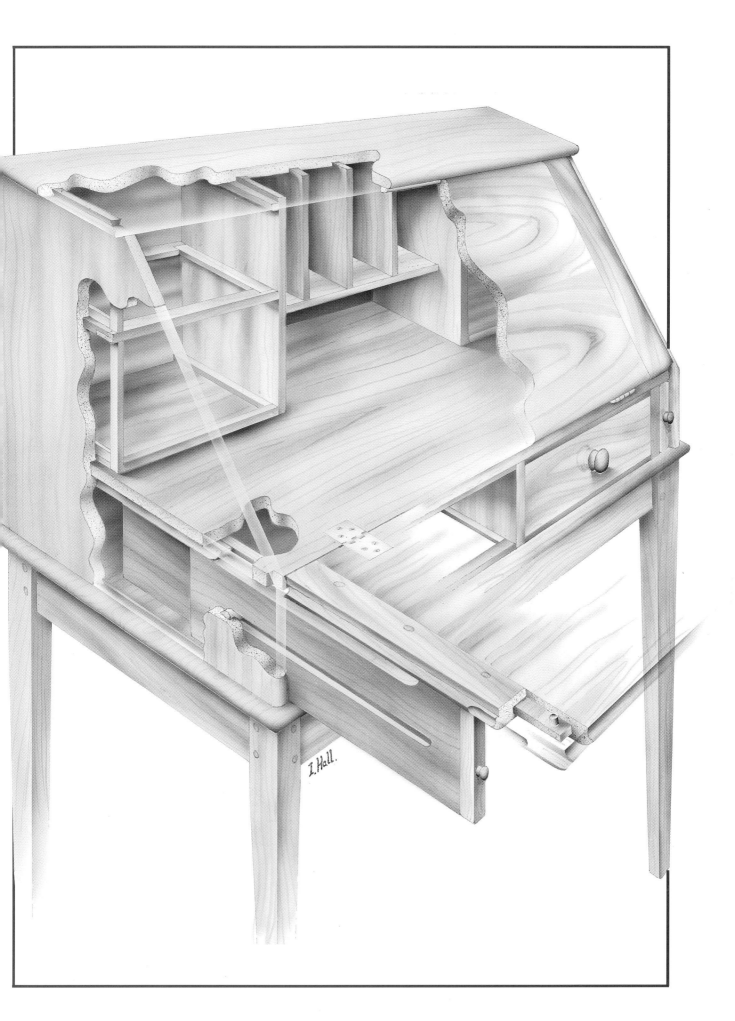

I. Hall.

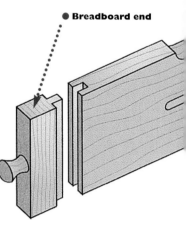

Dowel holes in tenon oval to allow movement

● Breadboard end

ABOVE: The bureau is attached to the stand with buttons screwed to the underside of the carcass

10mm ($^3/_8$ in) dowels are fitted into the carcass sides to act as stops for the lopers. Glue these into 15mm ($^5/_8$ in) deep holes, then file flats on their upper and lower surfaces until their thickness is 8mm ($^5/_{16}$ in) — this gives a larger surface area for the loper to run on.

Fall-front

The fall-front is a door when closed and a writing surface when opened, and as it is fixed on only one edge by hinges it must be constructed to stay flat. This is done by tenoning its ends into long-grain cleats, sometimes called breadboard ends, in such a way as it can shrink and expand without cupping.

Make up the main board to width as before then cut the tenons, forming a 22mm ($^7/_8$ in) shoulder at each end, *see fig 3*.

Cut mortices in the cleats leaving 25mm (1in) at each end; this gives a 3mm ($^1/_8$ in) gap at each end of the tenons to allow for expansion caused by humidity changes, *see panel*.

The dowel holes in the outermost ends of the tenons

should also be slightly ovular.

Dry-assemble and clamp the cleats to the fall-front, then from what will be the inner face drill dowel holes through the tenons and just into the outer cheek of the mortices, taking care not to break through the outer face. Dismantle, and elongate the dowel holes in the tenons to allow sideways movement.

The fall-front can now be assembled and dowels glued in position. The tenons must be free to slide along the mortices, so restrict the use of glue to no more than 50mm (2in) either side of the centre of the boards.

Next, clean up then cut a quadrant profile in the top edge, followed by the rebates and finger grips in the end cleats.

Fitting

Cut in and fit the hinges to the fall-front, then from these mark the hinge positions on the centreboard, cut in and check for correct alignment.

Slide the centreboard into place, refit the fall-front and make any final adjustments — do not glue the centreboard yet.

Lopers

The fall-front is supported when open by a pair of pull-out lopers. Like the fall-front, their end-grain is capped with breadboard ends for stability and appearance. To protect the face of the fall-front, a strip of felt or leather is glued to their top edge.

Each loper is sandwiched between the carcass side and the adjacent drawer divider. A dowel, *see above,* restricts travel.

Shape and cut two kickers — which also hold the dividers in position — a fraction wider than the thickness of the lopers, and glue and screw into place, *see fig 4.*

Install the lopers in position, then fix the dividers by pocket-screwing through them into the centreboard at the top; and with two screws driven up through the

• Tenon narrower than mortice

ABOVE: Fig 3 Construction details of fall-front. The correct construction technique for the fall-front is paramount because of the risk of movement warping the surface. The tenons are deliberately under-cut in their depth to allow for natural movement. The holes into which the dowels are placed to peg the cleats at either end are also ovular for the same reason.

• Kicker

ABOVE: Fig 4 Loper details and construction

• Dowel stop

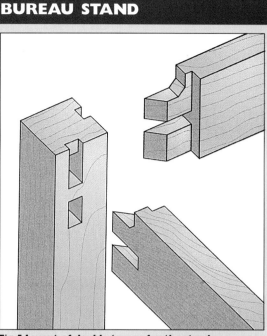

BUREAU STAND

Fig 5 Layout of double tenons for the stand

THE STAND is attached to the bureau by buttons screwed to the underside of its base, and located in grooves cut in the stand's rails, *see picture.*

The rails are joined to the legs using twin secret haunched mortice and tenon joints, *see fig 5.* Each of the joints is dowel-pegged, providing added strength and following the Shaker tradition.

The slender legs demand four lengths of even-grained, knot-free timber. Arrange each piece so that the run of the grain is from top to bottom, making for a cleaner finish when planing the tapers.

Tapering the legs on their inner faces sides avoids a pin-toed look; make sure that each taper begins below the mortice hole even after cleaning up; with a shallow angled taper like this even sanding its face can move its start position a surprising distance.

After the leg to rail joints have been glued up, drill holes for dowels through the tenons to a depth less than 35mm (1⁵⁄₈in), leaving a blind end. Cut a narrow groove along the length of each dowel to allow excess adhesive to escape, then glue and fit.

---

carcass at the bottom.

It will be seen from the illustration that the main drawers run between runners and rails which are planted onto the carcass bottom and under the centreboard. These components also form housings for the drawer dividers, the divider in the centre being fixed in the same way as the drawer/loper dividers.

The centreboard can now be glued, a stop for the fall-front then being fitted along the front of the top carcass member, *see main illustration.*

Interior

The arrangement of drawer and pigeon-holes in the upper part of the carcass comes next. Cut grooves in the main vertical dividers to accommodate the dust shelves and the base of the pigeon-holes, then slide them into place dry.

Now cut the pigeon-hole members and groove their base. Glue the vertical pieces to it; then when dry the assembly can be slid into position.

The two small drawer runner

frames are made using concealed half lap joints; when these attain a sliding fit all the components can be glued into place.

To compensate for any discrepancies, the runners, kickers and fillets are not fitted until after the drawers are made.

Drawers

I used cherry for the drawer fronts, but the sides, backs and bottoms are in sycamore (*Acer pseudoplatanus*). This gives the inside a light, clean-looking appearance which is enhanced by veneering the interior face of the drawer fronts in the same material.

The drawer knobs may be turned from wood as here, or can be of brass or china, all in keeping with Shaker tradition.

As the drawer bottoms are solid wood, they are fitted dry into grooves in the fronts and sides. These grooves are best cut before the dovetails, as the backs finish at the top of the bottoms to allow them to project

Remember that the grain of solid drawer bottoms must run across the drawer so that

shrinkage is in the front-to-back direction, and can be taken up by the overhang — for this reason the bottom is screw-fixed to the underside of the drawer back through an elongated slot. ■

● *Full dimensioned drawings and cutting list for this piece are available free to readers of F&C. Please send a stamped, self-addressed A4 envelope to: Shaker desk drawings, Furniture and Cabinetmaking, Castle Place, 86 High Street, Lewes, East Sussex BN7 1XN.*

Headboard head

Be warned – **Andrew Skelton**'s deceptively basic design for a bed will not induce sleep

MAIN PHOTOGRAPHY BY STEPHEN HEPWORTH

ANDREW SKELTON, who has been making high quality hardwood furniture for the past 15 years, was recently commissioned to make a copy of a seat at Charleston. The original seat no longer existed and the design was arrived at by studying photographs and a few seconds of film. Skelton trained as an architect and says furniture-making is a natural progression from that discipline. He lives and works in the Derbyshire Peak District.

T HIS DESIGN ATTEMPTS to reduce the bed to its simplest components of posts, rails and headboard, and yet express richness of both form and materials.

I often find that simple-looking designs require more work, and this project adds weight to that argument, the desire to express each component both structurally and decoratively requiring subtle proportion and attention to detail and workmanship.

Clearly, a bed can be made using simpler construction, but part of our role as designers must be to attempt to challenge and excite not just the viewer of the finished object but ourselves as makers, *see photo 1 and fig 1.*

> "Clearly, a bed can be made using simpler construction, but part of our role as designers must be to attempt to challenge and excite"

Construction

While not involving straightforward joinery, the bed itself is not difficult to make. The whole project consists of only eight joints, and making the curved headboard can be broken down into stages.

The headboard and footboard are assembled in the workshop and the long rails secured with knock-down fittings on site.

The slats on which the mattress sits are bought, ready-made, along with their end fittings. They are simple to fit and have proved very comfortable. The slats, made from laminated beech (*Fagus sp*) sprung to a gentle curve, are held by rubber fittings needing no more than holes drilled in the rails – there being no point in making work for the sake of it!

3-step mortice

I like legs set at 45°, and here I feel they give a logic and tension to the design. More importantly, the curved headboard – the only definite requirement of the client – flows naturally from the angled posts.

I have, perhaps, further complicated the joint between the posts and the rails by showing the knock-down fittings decoratively. Ply tongues or even biscuits could serve here, but I was worried they might not close with the knock-down fixing and that any racking of the bed would leave an unsightly open mitre.

The secret of success with this joint, *see photos 2,4 and 5 and fig 2,* is to machine up plenty of test pieces and keep altering the set-ups until everything is spot on.

The pockets – for they are hardly mortices – in the legs are cut with a router guided by a jig which fits over the corner of the legs, *see photo 6.*

RIGHT:
Photo 1
Simple it may be, easy it ain't – a curved, laminated headboard

che

Blocks create a platform at 45° on which the router can run, and fences and stops are added to determine the exact position and size of the mortice.

The three steps of the joint depend on the positioning of the fences and accurately setting the depth of the router cut. The bottom of the router cut must hit the leg exactly at the front of the rail, and this is where the test pieces are invaluable.

These test pieces can also be used to set up for the short tenons; remember to cut a 45° haunch top and bottom if the corners of the rails are to be rounded over.

Andrew Skelton   29 January 1997

Fig 1 Design for a bed

Knock-down

The best way to pull up this joint is to apply pressure at right angles to the leg. Having drilled the appropriate holes, I used threaded rod and 45° blocks to test fit and glue up the short rails, *see photo 7.*

The actual fitting is made from a long M6 machine screw with a nut epoxied into one side. Rather than standard nuts, I used threaded rod connectors; at 18mm long these provide a better gluing surface – I had to cut the ends at 45°, *see photo 8.*

Both ends of the fittings are hidden by 15mm diameter aluminium plugs; although these could be of wood, I like the contrast of the oak and polished metal, *see panel for how to make these.*

"I accept that this would make more sense for a small production run, but even for the one-off a mould like this is relatively quick and economic to achieve"

Headboard mould

The headboard is laminated from four layers of 3mm MDF with veneers on both sides formed over a mould in the vacuum press. Having already made a jig to cut the leg mortices, now an 850mm by 1600mm (32 by 60in) mould for the headboard must be constructed.

I accept that this would make more sense for a small production run, but even for a one-off a mould like this is relatively quick and economic to achieve.

I make a 9mm MDF template which I use when routing the 25mm (1in) chipboard ribs. The template provides not only the shape of the curve but also cut-outs for battens with which to keep the assembled ribs in registration.

BELOW LEFT:
Photo 2 Mortice detail with M6 holes for threaded rod connectors

BELOW MIDDLE:
Photo 4 Stepped and mitred tenon

BELOW LEFT:
Photo 5 The completed joint with decorative aluminium plugs fitted

TOP RIGHT:
Photo 6 Jig for morticing legs

MIDDLE RIGHT:
Photo 7 Blocks in place to assist gluing up

BOTTOM RIGHT:
Photo 8 Bolts and plugs for leg joints

If the ribs are routed neatly and assembled carefully, in line and square, then the mould can be used later as a jig to accurately trim the headboard, *see photo 11*.

The curve of the ribs must allow for the skin of the mould – in this case three layers of 3mm MDF – and also for the spring-back of the formed piece. Spring-back is difficult to predict, especially in a curve like this with many different radii of curvature.

I simply 'tighten up' the curves to exaggerate the difference between the highs and lows. My mould, which was 5mm higher and 5mm lower than the actual curve, proved to be a little tight – the panel didn't spring back as much as I had anticipated, *see photo 12*.

It still amazes me how rigid even three glue lines will make a laminated panel. To take the guesswork out of guessing, the serious and sensible student of laminating would of course keep a notebook of what happens when and where.

Easier life

The thought of having to use curved scrapers and hand-sanding the headboard filling me with horror, I veneered the two outer – oak (*Quercus robur*) for the back and burr oak for the front – sheets of 3mm MDF and cleaned them up while they were still flat.

This technique does have its limitations, however, making the substrate significantly less pliable and the complete package less rigid.

I first veneered a piece of 3mm MDF with the backing cross-grain oak and cleaned it up before gluing it over the mould to three further sheets of 3mm MDF. I then dimensioned and fitted the headboard, remembering that it was still short of its final layer of veneered MDF.

It is always difficult to cut curved panels true and out of wind, and I used the mould as a guide on which to run the router to cut the first straight edge. The other cuts to dimension the panel can be made on the saw bench from this straight edge.

The curved headboard will not enter a vertical groove in the posts for assembly, *see fig 2*. To circumvent this problem I cut these grooves oversize and made a tapered strip which I glued in during assembly.

The strip forces the panel nicely to the front of the groove and, once scraped flush, hardly shows – particularly as it is behind the headboard.

For extra security I used aluminium 4mm dowels pinned through the front and the groove at intervals down the posts. The bottom edge of the headboard is fixed to the back rail by a groove that is routed using one of the mould ribs as a template and a guide bush.

In order to allow for this groove, extra width is needed on the back rail;

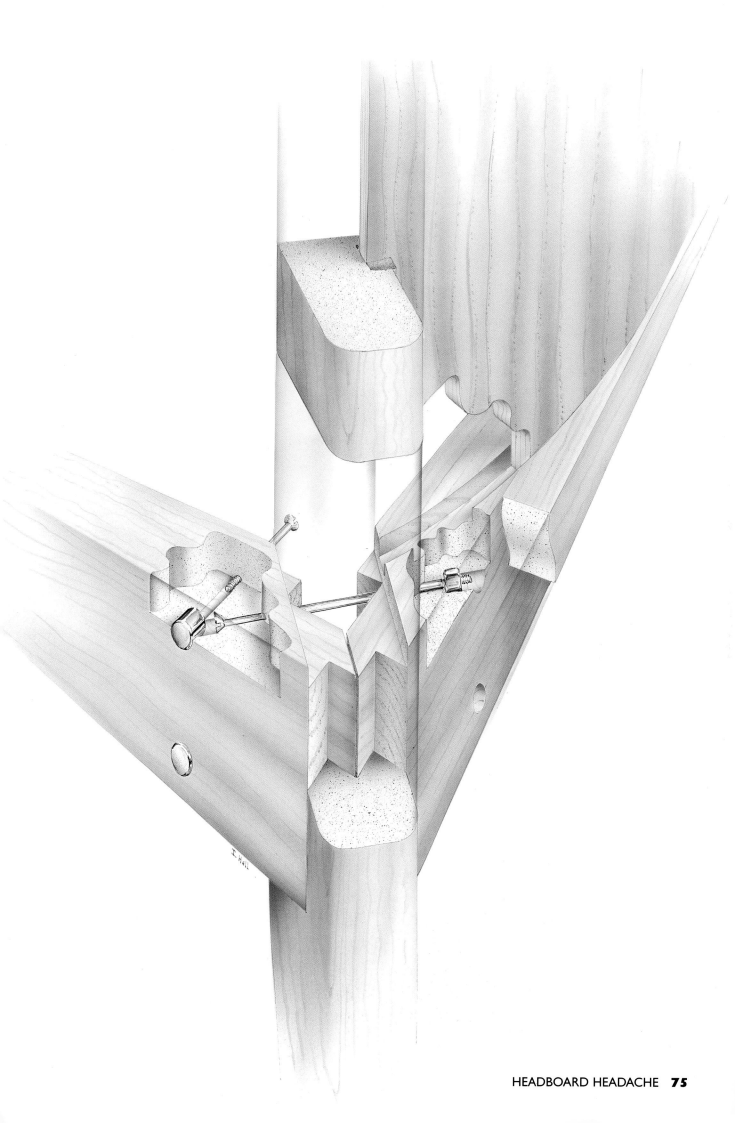

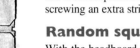

this is accomplished by gluing and screwing an extra strip to it, *see fig 3*.

Random squares

With the headboard carefully fitted, cut the outside piece of 3mm MDF exactly to size and draw on it the pattern for the burr oak face veneers. The random squares of burr oak are a deliberate attempt to use the veneer in a way that is modern, avoiding the connotations of the book-match or other traditional ways of laying veneer.

From a practical point of view, smaller, and cheaper, pieces of veneer can be used, but, set against that, cutting and taping 200-plus squares is not the quickest or most exciting of operations.

I glued this strange sheet – more tape than veneer – to the piece of MDF and sanded it carefully while it was still flat. This piece was then glued to the rest of the headboard

ABOVE: Fig 3 Plan view of leg assembly

ABOVE RIGHT: Photo 11 Headboard mould

BELOW: Photo 12 The completed curve

on the mould in the vacuum press – a tense and worrying operation as the two components now represented an incredible amount of time, effort and money.

Thankfully, all aligned properly and I was able to clean the edges of the complete assembly with a few strokes of a hand plane.

The top edge of the headboard is veneered with burr oak, and I used hot Scotch glue although there are other suitable methods.

I was careful to mask off the front and back to avoid glue runs negating all my 'pre' cleaning up.

The headboard is finished with a semi-gloss lacquer; to effect a contrast with this and the polished metal I brushed out the grain of the oak and waxed it. ■

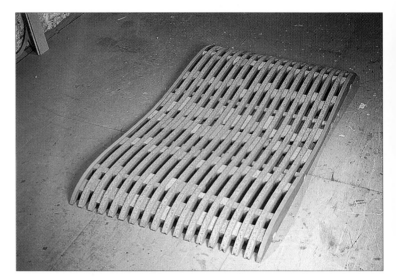

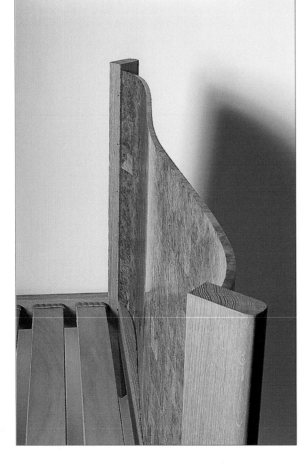

METALWORK FOR WOODWORKERS

Few woodworkers have fully equipped metalworking shops, but for anyone with a metalworking lathe then these little plugs present no problems. For those, like me, who don't have such equipment then a little bit of metalwork, especially in something as easy to work as aluminium, can be accomplished with woodworking tools.

I started with a piece of 9mm MDF, drawing lines to mark the centres before drilling 16 holes 15mm in diameter.

If the holes are tight enough then they will hold the aluminium bar while it is hacksawn off and thicknessed with files and belt sander to 9mm. Now the centre lines are re-drawn over the aluminium and the centres punched so that the plugs can be drilled and tapped, see *photo 9*.

I suppose this M4 screw to anchor the dowel is not strictly necessary, but it does ensure not being rung up and asked to replace a lost plug. With all the engineering work complete, the aluminium dowels, still held in the MDF, can be polished with a cotton mop in the pillar drill – if the dowels are pushed out slightly then the mop will give them a nice soft edge, see *photo 10*.

TOP LEFT: Photo 9 Threading plugs
LEFT: Photo 10 A nice shine and edge to the plugs

Walking the line

Laura Mays makes a prize-winning table

THIS TABLE is many things. It was the first real design-and-make project that I undertook as a second year student at the Furniture College, Letterfrack, County Galway in Ireland. It is also the table that earned me £200 worth of tools, a jigsaw, and a router, as joint third prize winner at the *F&C* competition at the 1997 Axminster Tool and Machinery Exhibition. And it is now the table that sits in the window of my parents' house in County Wicklow

The brief

The brief was: 'Frame making in solid timber'. It was to be a prototype for a bedside table, or a coffee table, to be made in a batch of 100 – although in my case that side of the brief was sidelined, and I concentrated on it more as a hand-crafted object.

It is a feature of the college that students take briefs differently, some adhering carefully to them, others using them as a departure point for pursuing their own interests. There are things to be said for each approach.

This particular table would not be suitable for a large batch, as became apparent in the making.

> "The table's spatial interest is lost when it is pushed up against a wall or a bed – it seems to need air on all sides"

Space and design

I designed what I thought was going to be a bedside table, but ended up as an occasional table. Its spatial interest is lost when it is pushed up against a wall or a bed – it seems to need air on all sides.

Initially, a square table seemed to be more interesting. The joints were of intrinsic importance in setting both the style of the table and the ease of making.

The design had to allow for movement of the timber and it had to be stable, but I didn't want to do anything too conventional. After all this was my first chance in college to do a bit of designing.

Lines and planes

I thought of separating out the structure from the surface that would support objects, making the structure into a line, and the surfaces into planes, which would be as separate as possible from the frame.

ABOVE: The influence of Eileen Gray crept into the table

LEFT: Following in the footsteps of Paul Klee – taking the line for a walk

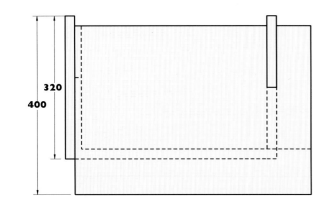

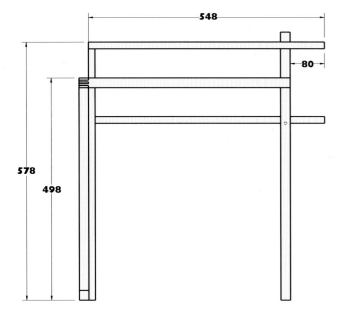

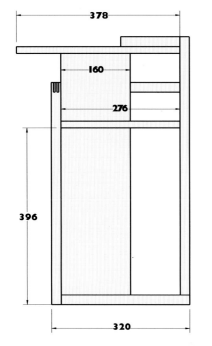

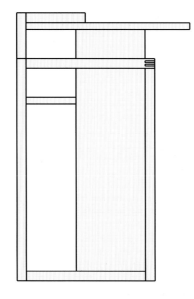

In the words of the artist Paul Klee, I 'took the line for a walk', defining some of the edges of a notional box. It seemed to make sense to further differentiate between the line and the plane by making them in two different woods that would contrast with each other, but not too much – a subtle contrast.

The wood

As it turned out there was a stock of lacewood (*platanus acerifolia*) in the college. I had never heard of such a timber, but because of its attractive name, I thought I'd take a look at it. It is from the plane tree, with similarities to both beech and sycamore, but with a lovely flickering-fleck figure when it is quartersawn – hence its name.

It goes well with cherry, which has more colour but is straighter grained. Any two similar, but different, woods might work just as well – beech and cherry, sycamore and beech, maple and cherry, or beech and maple.

Inspiration

Two tables by Eileen Gray, the modernist furniture designer, one of which is purely planes, the other mostly line, provided further inspiration. I wanted my table to have both plane and line. At this stage I was still thinking of it as a bedside table, and wanted to have a box with a flap-down door incorporated somehow into it – but this was soon abandoned as it was too much work, with not enough gain. After all, a second shelf does the same job.

Joints

In terms of joints, splined mitre joints were an option, but as the joints are taking a lot of load, it seemed to me that something stronger would be better – and there was ease of gluing up to think of.

ABOVE: Plenty of gluing area makes this joint both strong and attractive

Although I hadn't ever used one before, the spindle moulder seemed to be the answer – finger joints! Lots of gluing area, and good-looking.

A 22mm (⅞in) square section for the frame meant three fingers and two slots, or vice versa, of 4mm (¹¹⁄₆₄in) each for the inner ones, and 5mm (¹³⁄₆₄in) each for the outer ones, without using a wobble blade.

Expansion and contraction

The table is designed to allow for plenty of movement – the planes move together because the grain direction is the same in all of them. The top is slot-screwed from underneath to the part of the frame which wraps around over the top. A 6mm (¼in) steel bar ties the frame below the shelf. A slot is routed out of the underside of the shelf, allowing it to expand and contract independently of the frame.

Mock-up

Before starting to make the table, I made a very quick mock-up using MDF and white deal to check dimensions and sizes. The timber elements are brought to the smallest dimensions I thought I could get away with – I wanted it to look fine and delicate, but not too spindly.

BELOW: Lacewood provides a subtle contrast to the cherry

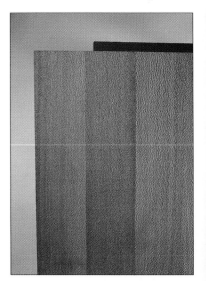

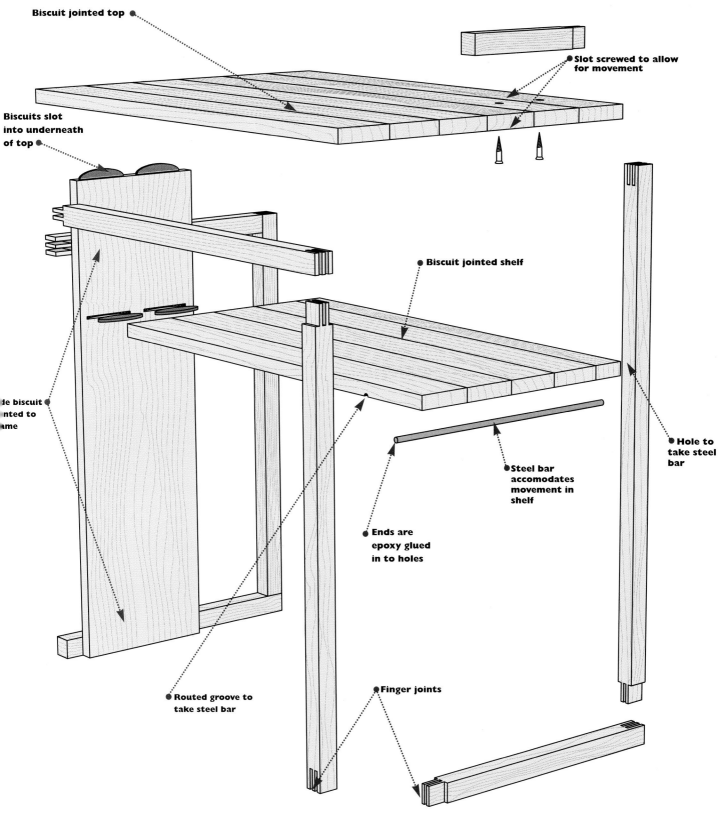

Biscuit jointed top

Slot screwed to allow for movement

Biscuits slot into underneath of top

Biscuit jointed shelf

...de biscuit ...nted to ...me

Hole to take steel bar

Steel bar accomodates movement in shelf

Ends are epoxy glued in to holes

Routed groove to take steel bar

Finger joints

Tops and shelves

Firstly the timber was selected on the basis of its grain and the overall quality of the board. Because only short lengths are needed, overall bowing or twisting are not the critical factors they would be in making a larger or thicker top. In fact, very little timber is used – there is just over a third of a cubic foot in the finished piece, but that's not including wastage. The top takes precedence over the rest when choosing boards.

The lacewood and cherry are planed and thicknessed – the cherry to 22mm (⅞in) square. The lacewood will end up at 15mm (¹⁹⁄₃₂in), but I left it over thickness, because in college we had the luxury of a speed sander that would take glued up panels to thickness – but this is not really necessary.

If care is taken when gluing up the panels, a quick skim with a jack plane should take out any small discrepancies in the biscuiting.

The panels are biscuited together, in strips of about 60mm (2⅜in).

This relatively narrow dimension should help stop any warping in the panels.

Everything is left overlength by 10mm (⅜in) or so. I try to cut pieces to length at the last possible moment, to allow for changes – but remembering to mark where the biscuits are so as not to reveal them when the panels are trimmed to length.

The glue is scraped off when it is still rubbery, and the surface is planed or sanded to level.

Cherry frame

The cherry is cut to length, and marked out for fingers or slots. I alternated them; that is, each piece had three fingers at one end and two at the other.

The spindle moulder is set up using slotting discs and all the three-fingered pieces run through – then the spindle moulder is adjusted for the two-fingered pieces.

This joint can alternatively be cut on a router table with similar slotting tooling designed for use in a router.

It is good to have a number of spare sections to practice on. The inside faces of the frame should be sanded at this stage as they will be harder to access after gluing up. The holes for the 6mm (¼in) steel bar should be drilled at this stage also, on a drill press preferably.

The biscuit slots for the connecting joints from the frame to the side and top pieces, can be cut now or when the frame is assembled. There are advantages to either – error is more likely if it is done now, but it is easier to clamp down the pieces.

Gluing up the frames

Now comes the fun bit, gluing up. Two people are more than twice as good as one – it is very handy to have someone else to hold the pieces while you tighten the clamps. I made little gluing blocks which pressed only on the fingers.

Clamps are needed in both directions to tighten the joints. If the joint looks a little open acrossways a small G-clamp can tighten it up.

A disadvantage of this table is that the joints are glued up sequentially, rather than all at once as in a conventional frame. This means the gluing up process is more protracted than it would otherwise be.

I used Cascamite which has a long clamping time, but aliphatic resin glue would do as good a job, and allow the whole process to be over much sooner. It is easier to glue up the two end frames flat, then go three-dimensional for the last one.

The joints are cleaned up using a block plane if necessary, and a scraper. The frame can then be sanded, through the grades of paper, at least to 240 grit.

Meanwhile, the lacewood panels are cut to length, biscuited, and the slot routed in the underside of the shelf for the bar. Then they can be glued into their configuration, the joints cleaned up if necessary with a plane, and sanded. During the assembly process the ends of the steel bar are glued into their holes in the frame with an epoxy resin like Araldite.

Finishing

The table is now ready for its final stage, oiling. I used Rustin's Danish oil,

EILEEN GRAY

Eileen Gray, the designer and architect, is now regarded as one of the pioneers of modern design in furniture.

She was born in Ireland in 1878. As a young woman she trained as a painter at the Slade school of art in London before moving to Paris, where she was to remain for the rest of her life.

Her interest in furniture began with a passion for Japanese lacquer work, which she studied under the master, Sagawara – later designing exotic pieces in the Art Deco style. She became known for her interior design and opened a shop in Paris.

In the later part of the 1920s however, her preoccupations shifted in a very different direction when she collaborated with Jean Badovici on an experimental house in the south of France, known as E1027, in which they focused on space and form, exposing the mechanics of the building, rather than disguising them.

Her work won the respect of some of the foremost modernists of the time, including the Swiss architect Le Corbusier, and the German avant garde group, De Stijl.

Modernists, at that time, were concerned with moving away from the lavish romanticism of Art Deco and were drawing on the influences of primitive art, Cubism, and the aesthetic of the machine.

They were interested in geometric forms, unadorned surfaces, exposed structure, and light and space. Minimalist perfectionism and love of flawless detail and proportions were of prime importance.

Eileen Gray's work was somewhat neglected during most of her life until in 1972, aged ninety three, she was appointed a Royal Designer for Industry. This prompted a resurgence of interest and new editions of her modernist furniture of the 1920s and 1930s were put into production.

There are examples of Eileen Gray's furniture in the collections of the Victoria and Albert Museum in London, and Musée des Arts Decoratifs in Paris – and drawings and models in the collection of RIBA in London.

but there are a number of equally good ones available. The oil is applied with a brush or a rag, and then the excess is wiped off before it dries. The rags should not be squashed together and thrown in a bin. They can self-ignite – my brother tells me he nearly set fire to his flat by leaving rags in a crumpled heap after oiling a table top.

Because the table had ended up on a wooden floor, I stuck little clear plastic glides on it. The oil needs to be scraped back through in order for the glides to adhere properly.

Assessment

The table has a definite De Stijl or Bauhaus look. It appears modern, and combines spatial interest with traditional values of solid timber and exposed joints.

The frame was not easy to glue up, a flat jig might have been a worthwhile expense of time.

If the weight of more than a few books is to be placed on the top, it might be worth looking at an additional support for it.

But, as soon as I finish a piece, I start thinking about how it could be

better and how I would do it differently the next time. I guess that's called the learning curve, but it's what keeps me going from project to project – enthusiastic to try out on the next, what was learnt on the last. ∎

BELOW: A steel bar provides the solution to the shrinkage problem

Cabinet Sauvignon

This neat wall cupboard would suit many purposes – here it stores **Bob Wearing**'s wine

THIS WALL CUPBOARD was made to accommodate the Wearing cellar, but it is a versatile form and could be easily adapted for service as, say, a bathroom cabinet or for general kitchen use.

A careful drawing needs to be made taking account of the intended contents, such as the height and number of bottles, the number and size of glasses and the choice of one or two shelves. Graph paper is useful for this kind of planning and a drawing produced on this will be quite good enough.

Approach

In this project the usual order of working is reversed - the curved door is made first, and only then is the carcass made to fit it.

If you decide to make a version with a flat door, then follow the usual procedure of carcass first, then the door to fit.

The door is built by laminating three layers of 3mm (⅛in) plywood. The two outer laminates are oak faced on one side only, though for convenience many will take all three layers out of the same sheet.

A mould is needed for this purpose, *see illustration*, I found that five ribs were adequate.

These ribs must be identical, and can be made so with perfect precision using a router. Softwood is quite satisfactory for these.

Former

First make a template, which can be approximately sawn from a plywood offcut which must be just thicker than the depth of your router's guide bush.

The curved edge of the template will be set back from what will be the finished size. To calculate the amount of this setting back, deduct the diameter of the chosen cutter from the diameter of the guide bush and divide the answer by two.

For example a 30mm guide bush, minus a 10mm cutter is 20mm; divided by two this gives 10mm. Thus the template must be 10mm behind the desired finish line.

This calculation becomes extremely messy if imperial and metric units are mixed; not recommended.

Pin the rib material to scrap plywood or blockboard and then pin the template on top.

The router is not going to sit nicely on such a small surface, so a 'levelling foot' is recommended, *see photo*.

With this setup it is easy to run round the template, just cutting into the scrap wood – repeat to make the five ribs. When they are ready, screw the ribs onto a blockboard or chipboard base from underneath.

The door

Apply glue to the inner faces of the outer two laminates, make the sandwich, hold together with a few strips of masking tape and place centrally on the mould.

If using PVA glue, work rapidly – Cascamite, Aerolite or Scotch glue all allow a bit more time.

If a vacuum forming bag is available this will do the job well, but it is not essential.

With such a shallow curve, three strong battens as shown will do. The central batten can be plain, that is,

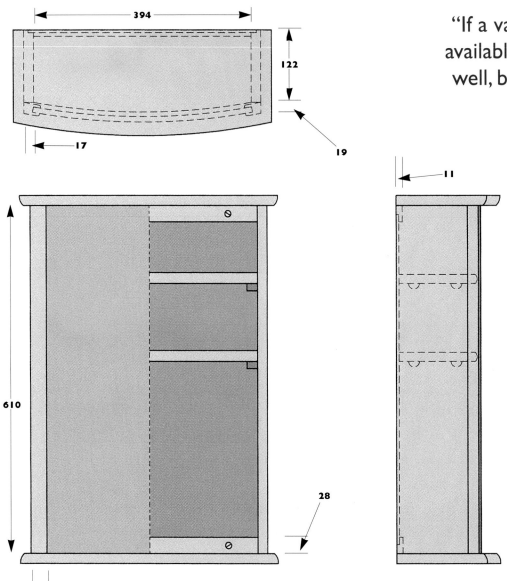

394

122

17

19

11

610

28

28

"If a vacuum forming bag is available this will do the job well, but it is not essential"

Carcass

Next prepare the sides, top and bottom.

The top and bottom must, at this stage, be over-wide. The exact shape will be scribed from the door later. The sides are made 6mm (¼in) longer than the inside height of the carcass, which will be dowelled together. Clearly mark the top, bottom, left and right sides, then the joints I, II, III & IV. The true faces are inwards and the true edges are to the rear.

Drill 8mm (⁵⁄₁₆in) dowel holes in the ends of the sides. Precise spacing is not necessary; 5 or 6 dowels will do.

Cramp a block, in turn, on the top and bottom, at the inner edge of the cabinet. Insert dowel marker pins in the two outer holes of a side, hold this tightly against the block, then tap smartly to give a marking.

Drill these two holes, ideally using a pillar drill or a drill stand if possible. Repeat on the other three corners.

Glue in the dowels, wash off surplus glue and saw off to length. Tap up joint No.1, then, with a sharp marking knife, scribe round to mark a housing. Remove the waste to a depth of 3mm (⅛in), then repeat for joints II, III & IV.

Arrange a small notch to the front corners of the sides to conceal the joints. When satisfied with the joints, insert dowel marking pins into the remaining holes, mark these centres and drill the remaining holes.

Trimming

Rebate the two sides only to accept a back panel of 6mm (¼in) oak faced plywood. If the cupboard is small, maybe the 3mm (⅛in) plywood already used will suit.

Prepare two hanging rails with stub tenons to fit the back panel rebates.

Using the same setting, rebate one edge of each for the back panel. Round over the inside corners of these then drill and countersink for hanging screws. Put three locating dowels into each.

Cut the back panel to fit but glue nothing at this stage.

Cramp the carcass up firmly without glue, then plane the door at its top and bottom to fit. Aim for a tight fit with a thin card under the bottom edge.

The next stage is important. Check how well the door sits on the two

square edged, but the two outside battens require planing to a slight angle in order to take the cramps well.

To stop slipping, add a few pieces of double sided tape. Cramp on the central batten, pull down and cramp at the sides.

Hinges will not screw to the plywood edge produced so two lipping strips are required. Make these strips over-wide to allow for fitting to the carcass, groove them to accept the panel, round over the inside corners and glue in place.

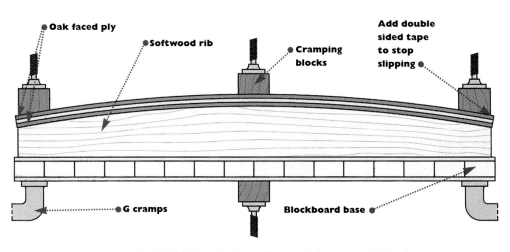

Oak faced ply

Softwood rib

Cramping blocks

Add double sided tape to stop slipping

G cramps

Blockboard base

ABOVE: Making the lamination, end view of mould for door

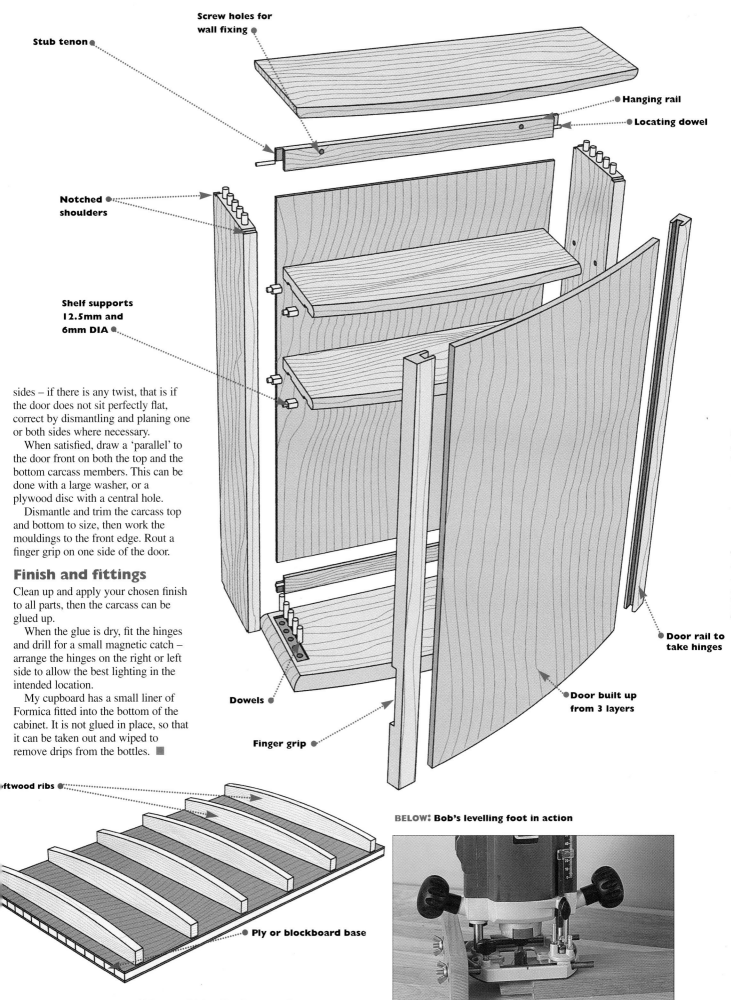

Stub tenon

Screw holes for wall fixing

Hanging rail

Locating dowel

Notched shoulders

Shelf supports 12.5mm and 6mm DIA

Door rail to take hinges

sides – if there is any twist, that is if the door does not sit perfectly flat, correct by dismantling and planing one or both sides where necessary.

When satisfied, draw a 'parallel' to the door front on both the top and the bottom carcass members. This can be done with a large washer, or a plywood disc with a central hole.

Dismantle and trim the carcass top and bottom to size, then work the mouldings to the front edge. Rout a finger grip on one side of the door.

Finish and fittings

Clean up and apply your chosen finish to all parts, then the carcass can be glued up.

When the glue is dry, fit the hinges and drill for a small magnetic catch – arrange the hinges on the right or left side to allow the best lighting in the intended location.

My cupboard has a small liner of Formica fitted into the bottom of the cabinet. It is not glued in place, so that it can be taken out and wiped to remove drips from the bottles. ∎

Dowels

Finger grip

Door built up from 3 layers

ftwood ribs

Ply or blockboard base

BELOW: Bob's levelling foot in action

ABOVE: The mould for the door panel

Round and ar

**ABOVE: Photo 1
The whole unit
open, showing the
position of the
carousel within**

**BELOW: Photo 2
Tambour doors
closed, discreetly
shielding all the
electronic
wizardry**

Sanity warning

THIS ARTICLE is about how I made a carousel to hold cassettes and CDs – but first, a word or two about the cupboard to help preserve the sanity of anyone trying to make something similar.

It seems that everyone, these days, wants to hide their television, video, hi-fi and extensive collection of records, cassettes, CDs and videos – in the smallest space possible!

This cabinet, *see photos 1&2*, is quite compact in relation to what fits inside – but is nevertheless 850mm (33½in) high and 1040mm (41in) long, each side of the L-shape.

The trouble is, these dimensions will not fit through the average door – unless you are remarkably lucky and can somehow feed it round.

I went to the trouble of cutting out a full size plan from a piece of hardboard to show the clients how little space the piece of furniture would take up – but I still didn't twig that I wasn't going to be able to get it into the room when it was 850mm rather than 3mm high.

Luckily this obvious fact – and inexcusable design error – dawned on me as I started cutting out the pieces for the cabinet.

As it turns out the design lends itself to being knockdown, because the two sets of sides are at right angles and brace each other. It was easy to make the carcass so that it can be assembled on site using

biscuits for location, and threaded fasteners to pull the joints up.

The other, and more serious, thing to watch as far as your health goes is the noxious dust from MDF and, of course, its weight – the carousel alone is pretty heavy!

Storage

The carousel, *see photo 3*, fits in the corner of the 'L' shaped unit and has eight bays, holding a total of 128 CDs and 102 cassettes – not bad in a space that would normally be inaccessible, and therefore wasted.

In the end the clients decided that they wanted a few videos in the carousel so I changed a bay of 32 CDs – to a bay of videos – a mere nine. I spent some time looking at a drawing showing a plan view of the cabinet and trying to optimise the useful sizes of the compartments.

As far as the carousel is concerned the aim is to make the diameter as large as possible, and not to restrict access by making the opening

ound

Andrew Skelton makes a carousel for CDs and cassettes

PHOTOGRAPHY BY STEVEN HEPWORTH AND ANDREW SKELTON

between the sides too small – a whole bay needs to be visible through the opening otherwise finding a selection might become very difficult.

Easy to read

To make the titles of the tapes and discs a little easier to read – the unit is on the floor – I tilted the shelves backwards – this also makes sure that things won't fall out as the carousel is spun.

Thought must also be given to how the discs and tapes are removed. A quick mock up will show you the best height and position of the shelves – I recessed the fronts so that it is easier to get hold of the disc or tape.

When you are happy with these dimensions draw a section to show the tilt and depth of the shelves and the position of the backs – and from this establish the depths of the two shelving units.

Armed with these measurements you can juggle the widths of the bays until you achieve the required balance between CDs and cassettes, or whatever.

Discs

The carousel consists of top and bottom discs separated by a square core with eight separate shelving units.

I wanted an obvious finger-hold to turn the carousel and so I made cogged discs at the top and the bottom, *see photo 4*.

Using an oversized piece of 18mm MDF I drew on the circle and divided the circumference to mark the centres of the holes. After drilling the holes – a flat bit works fine – I bandsawed through them just outside the line.

I then spun the disc, on its centre, on the router table to clean it up, *see photo 5*. The quarter-round and cove-mouldings of this, and the other discs, were run against a curved fence, again using a router table, *see photo 6*.

The core is simply 25mm MDF biscuited together – and biscuited to the top and bottom discs. With hindsight I think that I would rely on the shelving units to space the

Photo 3
The carousel out of its shell, bearings in the foreground

ANDREW SKELTON, who has been making high quality hardwood furniture for the past 15 years, was recently commissioned to make a copy of a seat at Charleston. The original seat no longer existed and the design was arrived at by studying photographs and a few seconds of film. Skelton trained as an architect and says furniture-making is a natural progression from that discipline. He lives and works in the Derbyshire Peak District.

discs, and replace the heavy core with a length of threaded rod to pull the whole unit together.

Shelves

The shelves don't need to be very strong, for they are braced against each other when the unit is assembled, but simple dowels seem to make a surprisingly robust unit. I used 9mm MDF for the uprights and 12mm MDF for the shelves joining them with 6mm dowels.

Now, putting a tight fitting 6mm dowel in the edge of 12mm MDF will split it, so it is important that the hole gives the right fit. I tried the various 6mm drills I had but they were all too tight, so in the end I ground down a ¼ inch bit.

To do this simply roll the drill bit carefully against a grindstone trying to reduce its diameter slowly and evenly.

The holes we are drilling are not very deep, so there is no need to grind the whole length of the drill – just concentrate on the end, and keep drilling test holes.

You may, incidentally, decide to use a tighter drill in the sides which will not split.

Drilling dowels

My morticer has a Jacob's chuck, and although the casting that normally holds the mortice chisel gets in the way, I find it the quickest

BELOW: Plan of cabinet

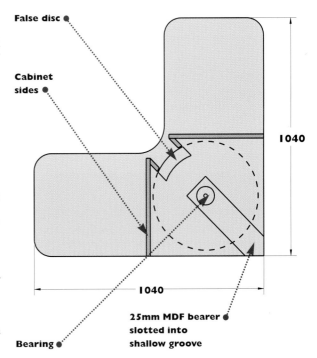

False disc

Cabinet sides

1040

1040

Bearing

25mm MDF bearer slotted into shallow groove

ABOVE: **Photo 4 Cogged discs top and bottom allow easy turning of the carousel**

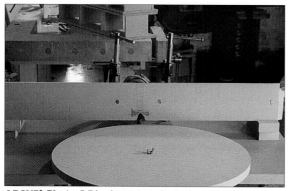

ABOVE: **Photo 5 Disc is centre pivoted with a bolt and wing nut to the router table, to ensure a true circle is cut**

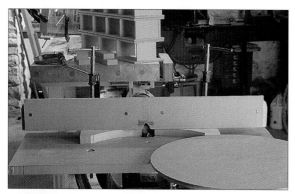

ABOVE: **Photo 6 A curved fence is set up to cut the coves and mouldings on the discs**

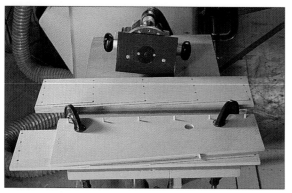

ABOVE: **Photo 8 Router with guide bush and template is used to cut the grooves for the backs**

and most accurate way of drilling dowels, *see photo 7.*

A pillar drill will do, of course, but the morticer has all the adjustments and stops to hand as well as a rugged cast fence.

The groove for the 2mm MDF backs has to be cut to the backward slope of the shelves. I used a router with a guide bush which follows an angled MDF template, *see photo 8.* The front edge of the side is located against a fence – this is doweled on so that it can be flipped over for the other hand – and the jig is lined up with each shelf by sighting through a hole.

A dowel stop indicates the bottom of the cut which is run out through the sides so that the backs can be slid in, after the unit is painted.

Fitting

When the shelves are assembled they can be put together between the discs – and the filling pieces, with their angles taken from the drawing, can be tried – note that the angles of each edge are different.

With everything correctly in place mark the position of the filling pieces and use this line to position the screw blocks. These blocks should be located a touch back, so that when the filling pieces are screwed in, they pull the whole unit together around its circumference.

I screwed through the sides of the shelves into the filling pieces to

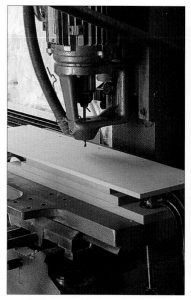

ABOVE: **Photo 7 Morticer fitted with a chuck for drilling the dowel holes for the joints that hold it all together**

ensure all was firm, but I don't think this was entirely necessary.

The carousel slides into the cabinet from the back. Its bearings are held in broad pieces of 25mm MDF which fit into shallow grooves in the top and bottom of the cabinet and are secured with screws. The exact height of the unit is critical, and adjustment can be made by planing down the pieces which hold the bearings.

OVER ENGINEERED

I was amazed how easily and truly the finished unit spun, and although the gap at the top and the bottom is only a millimetre, the carousel does not catch, even if you push on it.

If I were to make the unit again I would use less MDF in the core and discs, but I would stick with the robust bearings.

The bottom bearing is the most important and I used a tapered thrust bearing that comes from somewhere in a Land Rover, whilst the top bearing is a simple sealed example, see photo 9.

I got an engineer to make me a couple of discs with spigots to fit each bearing. They should be a tight fit in the bearing so that they do not turn – an engineer's fit – where you have to hit it sharply with a hammer and block to enter it and know that once on, it's a waste of time trying to remove it.

ABOVE: **Photo 9 Land Rover parts come in handy for furniture-making!**

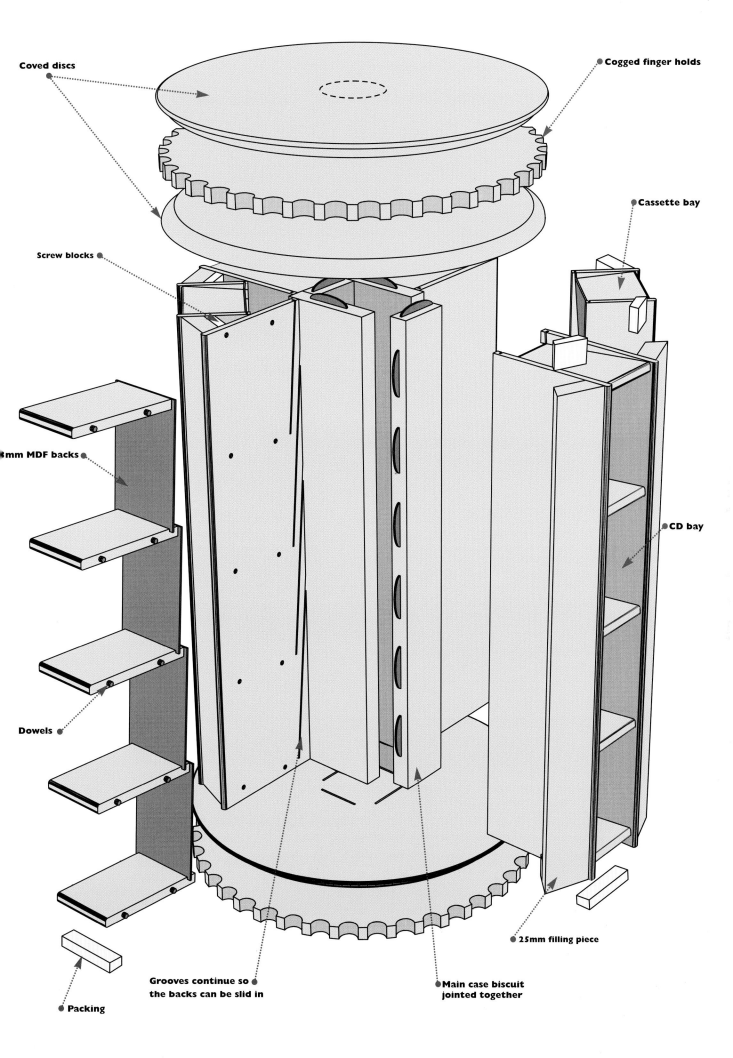

Coved discs

Cogged finger holds

Screw blocks

Cassette bay

3mm MDF backs

CD bay

Dowels

Grooves continue so
the backs can be slid in

Main case biscuit
jointed together

25mm filling piece

Packing

Finishing

I like painted finishes and enjoy the contrast of uniform colour and smoothness with the variety and texture of solid wood. I also think that a painted finish helps to smarten up the inside of a cupboard like this – where there are so many and varied things crammed in. But be warned, it is a time-consuming and mercilessly critical finish!

I suppose you could make this unit in perspex or in birch ply, and make a feature of the laminated edges, but I feel MDF is the ideal material.

There are many different finishes that can be applied to MDF but it particularly lends itself to painting.

For me, the two requirements of

> "Be warned, it is a time-consuming and mercilessly critical finish!"

a good, and trouble-free finish are proper preparation and a trip to the car body shop suppliers.

As far as possible all the edges should be sanded before assembly to at least 180 grit and care should be taken not to damage the surface of the MDF.

Now, with the shelf units assembled, but without their backs, go over everything and fill any dents or gaps – heaven forbid! – with car body filler.

After a final sand I prime all the edges with spray putty, thinned so that it can be brushed on. Spray putty has a very high solids content and, after a few thin coats and a fine sand, the edges should be smooth and shiny.

Next I spray everything with a coat of spray putty, and then spray the paint.

If you're looking to do a really good job, you can now spray a protective clear lacquer and cut back with buffing compounds – although this is not really appropriate for this job.

I use a not particularly good HVLP spray gun, and long for, but cannot justify, a top-of-the-range set up. However such equipment is not really necessary, as you can buy any colour of spray putty and lacquer in aerosol cans. ■

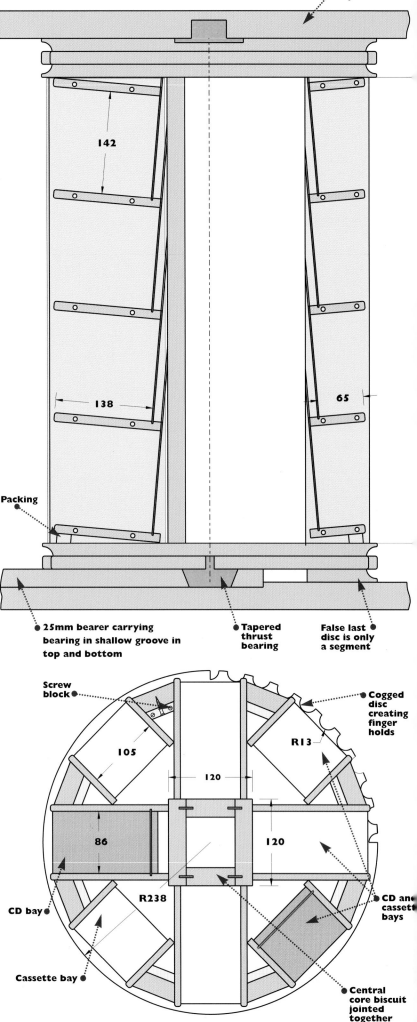

Top of cabinet

142

138

65

Packing

25mm bearer carrying bearing in shallow groove in top and bottom

Tapered thrust bearing

False last disc is only a segment

Screw block

Cogged disc creating finger holds

105

R13

120

86

120

CD bay

R238

CD and cassette bays

Cassette bay

Central core biscuit jointed together

Off-cut screen

Sean Feeney makes a folding screen in cocobolo and ash

● SEAN FEENEY trained at Rycotewood College from 1974 to '76. He worked as a pattern maker in industrial design before setting up Sean Feeney Furniture in '79. His designs are produced with the help of two assistants and three dogs in the wilds of Warwickshire

THIS SCREEN EVOLVED from my resolution to utilise several parcels of off-cuts and left-over boards that I had from a number of previous commissions. The reason was twofold: to create the ever-needed space in our timber sheds, and to ease my conscience by using these valuable natural resources.

Dilemma

I found myself left with a collection of short sappy lengths, slab cut tops of logs, and split and shook centre boards of cocobolo (*Dalbergia retusa*) – which is both expensive and rare.

These were the left-overs from two logs of about 45 cubic feet lying in stick, and home to all and sundry of the insect world in a corner of my shed since the completion of a 16 foot long table and dining-room suite that I made in 1986.

From a more recent commission, were several short lengths and ends of boards of English ash (*Fraxinus spp*), and a parcel of 50mm (2in) wide 2.8mm (⅛in) constructional veneers, which had been unused in the lamination and construction of eight dining room chairs.

The question was, how could all these bits and pieces be put to the best use?

Design

I had had the design of the screen in the back of my mind for some time, thinking that it would compliment the bedroom furniture which we were involved in designing and making in sycamore (*Acer pseudoplatanus*) and ash (*Frazinus spp*). I decided that the combination of ash and cocobolo would harmonise with the contrasting colours of the existing pieces.

The screen

All the jointing involved within the three frames is mortice and tenon, with the exception of the top rails which are haunched, enabling the corner stile detail to be removed.

The stiles have 8 by 2mm (⁵⁄₁₆ by ¹⁄₁₆in) channels to house the ash slats – which is achieved by using a scoring blade on a circular saw to prevent unnecessary wastage of 2mm router cutters!

Rails

The top and bottom rails have a concave-shape detail between the muntins, or vertical divisions, which is bandsawn to remove the stock and internally radiused, using a bobbin sander.

The inlay details of mother of pearl are 10mm (⅜in) in diameter and approximately 3mm (⅛in) thick, and

are glued with epoxy resin, filled and sanded flush.

Lamination

The laminated detail supporting the solid shaped top rail is constructed from 1mm (¹⁄₁₆in) thick cocobolo lamins, circular sawn and wide belt sanded to thickness – and subsequently bent in their middle on a double bass bending iron, prior to gluing around a male mould, using epoxy resin.

Assembly

All three frames are dry assembled and hinged together to ease the otherwise difficult task of accurate alignment.

The components are then polished, using French polish throughout and left to harden for two weeks.

The frames are glued together initially along their length, sashed cramped top to bottom, then across the width, finally adding the bent laminated top section.

Veneer

Having only several square metres of 50mm (2in) wide 2.8mm (⅛in) thick constructional veneer, I made the shortfall up by using off-cuts of ash boards which were sawn into 3mm (⅛in) strips. These, together with the veneer were thicknessed on a wide belt sander to a finish of 1.8mm (¹⁄₁₆in), cross-cut to the length required to fit within the framework.

I then polished both faces using a 50% sheen waterborne clear lacquer.

> ## "I decided that the combination of ash and cocobolo would harmonise with the contrasting colours of the existing pieces"

RIGHT: Detail of woven slats

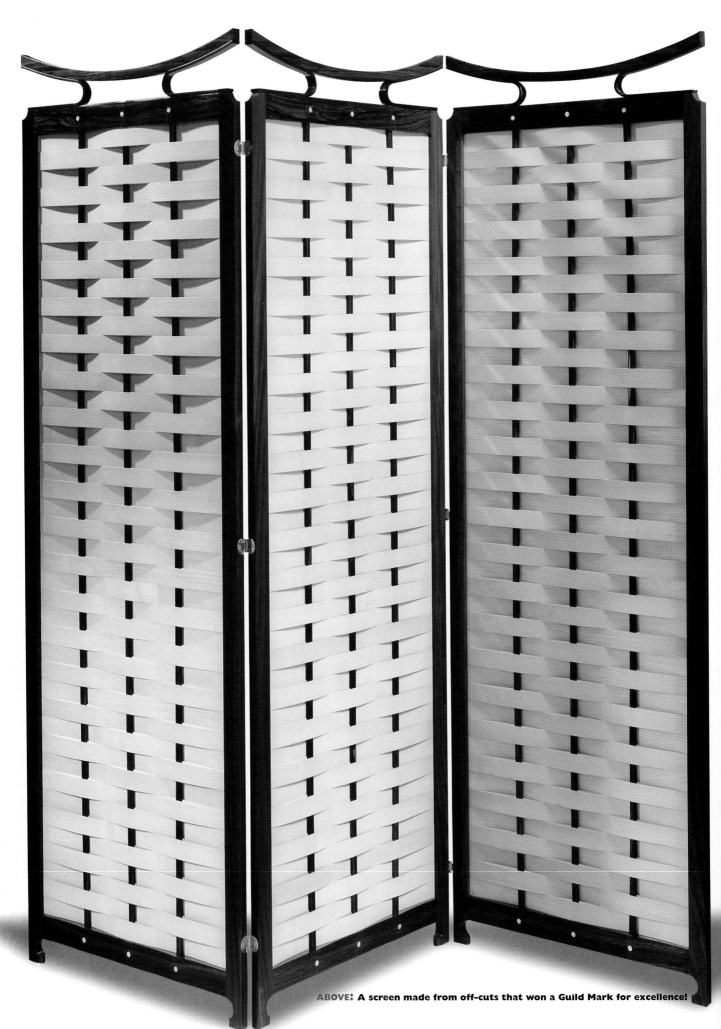

ABOVE: A screen made from off-cuts that won a Guild Mark for excellence!

Weaving

After several days, the slats were woven within the framework, occasionally using a bending iron to facilitate the insertion within a 2mm (⁵⁄₁₆in) channel in the frame stiles.

The frames are re-hinged back together and the cocobolo surfaces are burnished.

Conclusion

I exhibited the screen at the Celebration of Craftsmanship exhibition at Cheltenham in 1997 and was awarded a Guild Mark from the Worshipful Company of Furniture Makers for excellence of craftsmanship and design – a successful conclusion to a pile of off-cuts! *Sean Feeney also won first prize in the professional category of the 1997 F&C competition at Axminster for this spendid piece!* ▪

"I made the shortfall up by using off-cuts of ash boards which were sawn into 3mm strips"

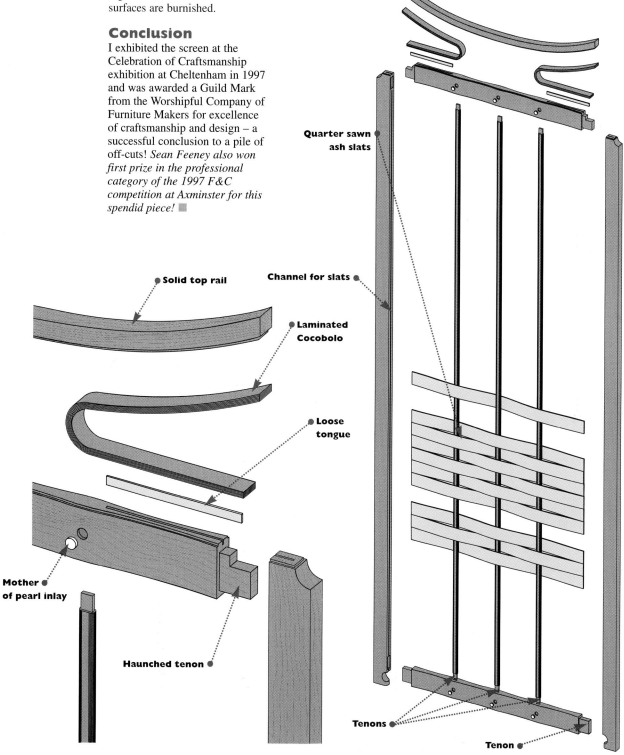

Quarter sawn ash slats

Solid top rail

Channel for slats

Laminated Cocobolo

Loose tongue

Mother of pearl inlay

Haunched tenon

Tenons

Tenon

Mike Cowie tries to improve on his original design for an Arts and Crafts-style writing desk

Second

PHOTOGRAPHY BY STEPHEN HEPWORTH

MIKE COWIE turned to cabinetmaking after redundancy. He took a City and Guilds furniture-making course, aligning this with a great deal of additional, unpaid, work to achieve a reasonable standard which led to self-employment. He says he sometimes doubts his sanity in entering such a fickle profession, but relishes the challenge of trying to meet his own high standards. Currently working from a converted garage, he is aiming towards a dedicated workshop/showroom.

ABOVE: Functional and simple Gustav Stickley-based design

Construction

English oak (*Quercus robur*) is used for the main carcass. The sides are cut from two wide, adjacent boards so as to achieve a bookmatch effect and avoid having joints showing on the front.

The top can be made from a nicely figured single piece, or, as I did, jointed and made up from three pieces.

After marking a line on the board, cut the taper freehand on the tablesaw. Both sides are then placed together and planed to size.

The shelves are jointed from narrower stock, trimmed square to size, the tenons are marked and cut, and the waste is chiselled out.

> "Normally, because I'm constantly trying to reinvent the wheel, I don't hold hard and fast to anything, but trying to mark joints without my cheap utility knives – no thank you!"

Marking joints

Using a sharp knife, the tenons can now be marked directly against the sides. Normally, because I'm constantly trying to reinvent the wheel, I don't hold hard and fast to anything, but trying to mark joints without my cheap utility knives – no thank you!

Transfer the lines around the outside, preferably with a marking gauge, slightly undersize to allow for final paring back to size. Chop out the mortices, relieving the waste with drill or router if preferred. Dry fit the sides and shelves together and mark the position of the mortices on the top, repeating the procedure until the carcass starts to look the part.

ARTS AND CRAFTS STYLE holds a particular attraction for me. I like its slightly softened angularities aligned with visible joints which provide ample opportunity to practise, so improving skills.

Unfortunately being unable to photograph the original writing desk – which sold for £750 – the only solution to illustrating this article was to make another one.

Now, this should have been a matter of simply getting out the drawings and measurements, and starting work; however, because I usually work only to a rough sketch – and in this case didn't even have that – my shortcomings came to the fore.

This piece was developed from an original that I had seen photographed in an old book about Gustav Stickley. The following is the result…

… And I have to say it was actually quite pleasant building something a second time, for I was able to attempt to correct the errors made first time round and change small details, hopefully for the better. The job took me 45 hours to complete.

draft

Stopped grooves

Using a router with a suitable bit, run a stopped groove down the inside back of the sides for the back panel and on the lower shelf.

While apart, a stopped groove also has to be cut on the underside of the top to take the back panel. The top has an undercut chamfer of 30°; this is cut on the tablesaw and finished with a hand plane.

> "The semi-circular cut-out on the sides is achieved with the aid of a suitable-sized dinner plate and bandsaw!"

The semi-circular cut-out on the sides is achieved with the aid of a suitably sized dinner plate and bandsaw!

With the router, drill an 8mm hole for the door pivot. The sides, shelves and top can now be cleaned up prior to gluing; finish to 240 grit. If the top tenons are to be chamfered, this is best done before assembly.

Padauk wedges

Padauk (*Pterocarpus sp*) wedges inserted diagonally into side tenons provide a nice visible effect which requires the tenons to be sawn to fit. To ensure squareness, glue up after checking by measuring diagonally.

I cheated at this point, placing scrap wood over the tenons and cramping them together. I glued up and left the carcass for half-an-hour before removing the cramps and inserting the wedges – happily,

without problem.

Cleaning up is a simple matter of leaving the glue until it is rubbery, and peeling it off with a sharp chisel.

Inner linings

I made my inner linings from 7mm (⁹⁄₃₂in) and 5mm (¹³⁄₆₄in) chestnut (*Castanea sativa*), this being ripped down from thicker stock and jointed to width. The original had square sides and drawer fronts, but this time I thought that an incline to match the slope of the sides would improve the look.

The carcass is dovetailed, and the shelves and partitions are all run in 4mm (⁵⁄₃₂in) grooves with the aid of the router. Using a router guide rail system for this task eradicates the need for straight-edges and clamps, so conforming to the KISS system (keep it simple stupid!).

> "Using a router guide rail system for this task eradicates the need for straight-edges and clamps, so conforming to the KISS system"

LEFT: Interior layout with sloped drawers matching the line of the front

BELOW: Padauk wedges are set diagonally into side tenons and 'dinner plate' semi-circular cut-out

BOTTOM: Chamfered top tenons

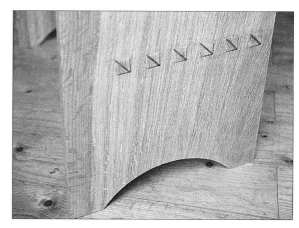

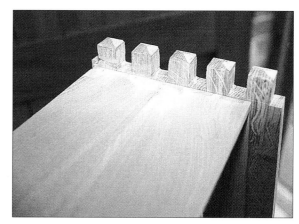

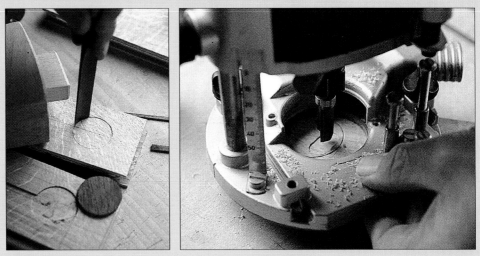

ABOVE: That essential workshop aid, the pepper pot, is used to mark out the inlay design

MIDDLE: Carefully cutting round the circle before routing out

RIGHT: Routing out waste

I commandeered a pepper pot which conformed to the radius of a suitable gouge – 20mm (¾in).

My method for cutting out the waste was to tap the chisel around the circle to the depth of approximately 2mm, then, using the router freehand with a 10mm flat-bottomed bit and setting it to a 2mm depth of cut, to rout out the waste – carefully!

Using a ruler and utility knife, trim down the length of the stem and, with a 4mm bit set to 2mm, trim out the waste as far as possible, finishing with a 3mm chisel.

The foot is cut out by hand. Trim some padauk to size and inlay into the recess, gluing it into place; clean up with plane and scraper, taking care that the padauk does not bleed into the oak.

Drawers, back panel

Mark off and cut all the sides of the angle-fronted drawers to the correct angle, and mark the dovetails in pairs to keep symmetry for the through dovetails. These are also cut together from quarter-sawn oak, the through dovetails keeping the thickness of the front down to 10mm (⅜in).

The drawer sides are thick enough to cut a groove for the cedar of Lebanon (*Cedrus libani*) drawer linings. A stop is glued underneath the drawer, and the handles are whittled from some padauk off-cuts, then drilled and screwed on.

The back panel is constructed from 10mm (⅜in) chestnut, rebated and chamfered to give a V groove effect. It is fitted into the groove at the top and drilled and screwed to the two lower shelves.

Door

All that remains now is the door. As the most visible part, it is worthy of some nicely figured wood, but I have to confess to running out of 25mm (1in) boards, and had to rip some 12mm (½in) down into 3mm, veneering this onto 15mm MDF for the inner panel.

I comforted myself with the thought that this was all for the best, as the movement of solid wood in a tightly held panel would only cause problems later.

Cut the frame to size, mortice and tenon the joints and dry fit together to measure for the inner panel size.

Cut the five inner panels to size and groove all inner edges to accept a 6mm (¼in) spline. Before gluing up, mark the outline for the decorative inlay, *see panel*.

After inlaying, glue the frame together and clean up. Use the router again to insert a ball catch into the door – a small collection of router bits can be surprisingly useful when needs must!

ABOVE: Dry-fit assembly of carcass

RIGHT: Construction of interior carcass and divisions

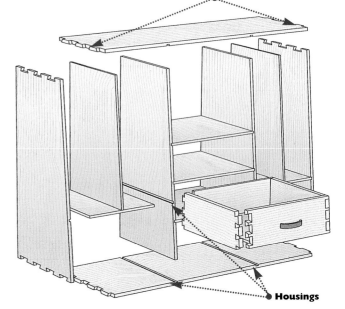

Dovetails

Housings

TOP: Sliding chestnut interior
divisions into housings

ABOVE: Complete interior carcass
assembled and being tried for fit

BELOW: Top with 30° chamfer
ready for assembly – note
mortices

ILLUSTRATION BY IAN HALL

Hinging

Unable to purchase hinges of the kind used originally on this type of desk, and without the time to construct them, I decided to use a simple pivot via an 8mm brass or aluminium bar or rod inserted into the hole previously drilled and epoxied into place.

Use the router to cut a mating groove on the sides of the door panels again. This procedure unfortunately leaves a very weak point, as I know to my cost, so to counter this a brass plate is inset and screwed into place – again with the help of the router. How long jobs would take without this versatile tool I can't say – I haven't the time to find out!

Additional security can be achieved by the use of a chain secured to the door and sides to restrict movement.

The door handle is whittled from a piece of oak and glued into a rebate cut into the door. The handle's concave underside allows a good grip.

I had intended cutting off the through tenons on the sides flush, as on the first piece but, because they looked quite neat, I trimmed the wedges and chamfered the tenons, leaving them 3mm (⅛in) proud. I have found that these 'sticky out bits', as they have been described, fascinate people, which is all to the good.

Finishing

After cleaning up, the desk can be finished with sanding sealer, rubbed down and waxed, so producing, to my mind, a lighter, cleaner look than that which results from my usual oil finish.

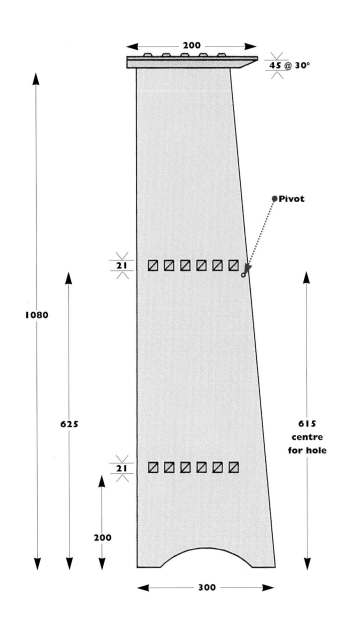

ABOVE AND OPPOSITE PAGE: Side, top and front elevations

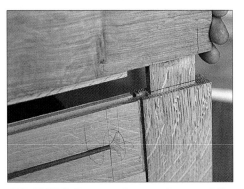

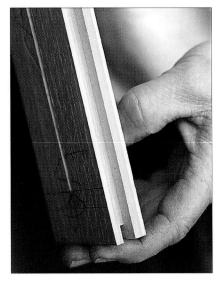

FAR RIGHT: Close up of groove for one of the segments of the inlaid door panel

RIGHT: Drawers awaiting handles

ABOVE: Vital dry fit of tenon and spline on door panel

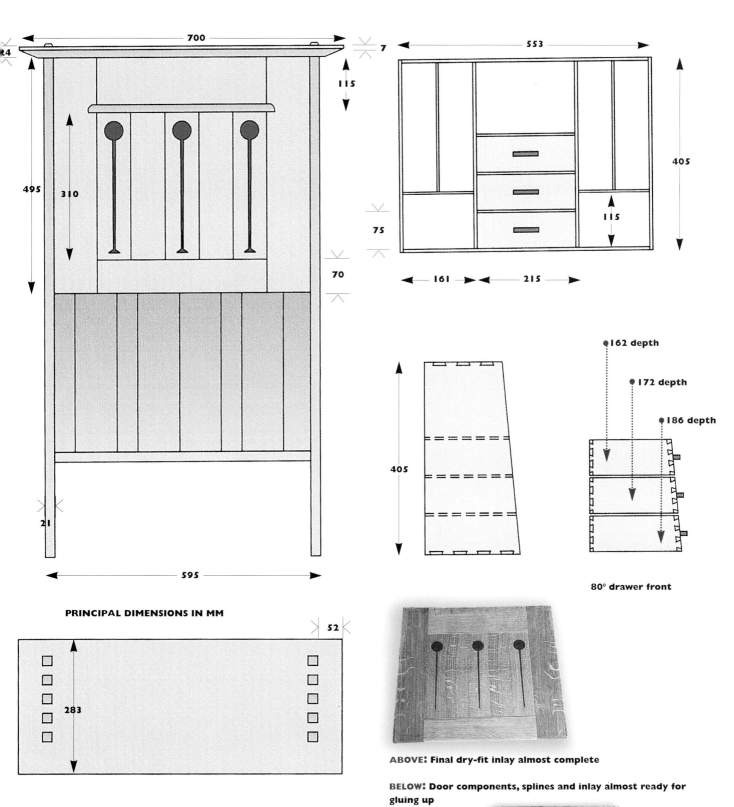

700

24

7

115

495

310

70

21

595

PRINCIPAL DIMENSIONS IN MM

52

283

553

405

75

115

161

215

405

162 depth

172 depth

186 depth

80° drawer front

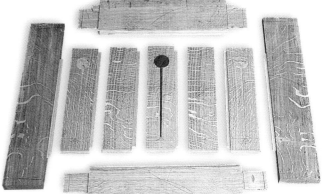

ABOVE: Final dry-fit inlay almost complete

BELOW: Door components, splines and inlay almost ready for gluing up

SNAP TO IT

Every maker has a personal preference for marking knives. Because they are cheap and no sharpening is involved, I favour the type of utility knife which is fitted with snap-off blades.

The routing was accomplished with a Festo 900E. I find its one-handled design quick to set up and, when used with the FS 800 guide rail system, extremely versatile, often avoiding having to set up complicated fences and jigs.

DeWalt's guide rail system, which complements their complete range of routers, works in a similar fashion.

Wrestling with

With a nod to David Savage, **Mike Cowie** makes an Arts and Crafts-inspired chest of drawers

MIKE COWIE turned to cabinetmaking after redundancy. He took a City and Guilds furniture-making course, aligning this with a great deal of additional, unpaid, work to achieve a reasonable standard. He says he sometimes doubts his sanity in entering such a fickle profession, but relishes the challenge of trying to meet his own standards. Currently working from a converted garage, he is aiming towards a dedicated workshop/showroom.

AN ADVANTAGE of self-employment – which admittedly can mean some lean times – is that personal preference can be exercised in the choice of a particular piece to be made under the guise of a display item or simply to improve quality.

This chest of drawers was inspired by one made by David Savage in sycamore and English cherry.

Timber, design

Initially the whole was to be constructed from sycamore (*Acer pseudoplantanus*), a wood which I feel is terribly undervalued – though mercifully cheap! I felt, however, that too much of it in such a large piece would probably have looked too bland, and I would have opted for American cherry (*Prunus serotina*) as a contrast for the drawer fronts had this timber been available in very wide section.

Instead I substituted its English cousin (*Prunus avium*), using this wood for the first time. On first impressions this seemed a little subdued due to the flashes of green within, though on finishing with oil the colours radiated out.

The length of sycamore on hand determined the overall height, and a quick sketch offered a pleasing width that,

RIGHT: Pale sycamore sides understate the size of this chest of drawers and add subtlety

BELOW: Detail of English cherry coving separating plinth and carcass

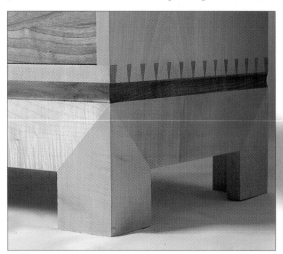

ctangles

though not quite in concert with the Golden Section, *see panel*, was pleasing nonetheless. Rules are made to be broken!

I decided to give the chest an Arts and Crafts look by virtue of dovetailed sides with through mortice and tenon bearer rails; and while this looks good, and has drawn many positive comments, it was a bit of a devil to put together, *see below*.

Preparation

I cut the sycamore to size, planed and butt-jointed it with the aid of the Plano clamping system, a really excellent performer and to my mind a must for the professional or committed amateur.

When dry, the glued up boards are cleaned up with a finely set No 4 plane, marked to size and squared off with a Festo portable saw and guide rail; this is simple to use and a whole lot cheaper than a dimension saw!

A feather cut with a plane is made on the edge to eradicate any saw marks and ensure squareness. Dovetails are marked and here, because I am as yet unable to cut dovetails by eye, I found an aluminium dovetail square useful.

Against convention, the tails are placed on the long sides of the carcass for visual effect.

Jointing

Cutting the tails requires the assistance of some two-by-two battens clamped to the board to reduce chattering.

When possible I cut dovetails on

the bandsaw, but in this case I was glad of my £1.99 gent's saw. This tool is positive with a fine kerf, but I am experimenting with a Japanese dovetail saw and am as yet undecided.

Problems ensued in marking out the pins; trying to balance a 1110mm (54in) length of timber steadily in a confined space while scribing gives the air of a pantomime.

For accuracy, the through tenon positions were marked from a rod.

These mortices for these were cut from both sides, first using a router to cut away the majority of waste and then paring back to the line with a chisel.

To ensure accurate repeat cuts, the bearer rails were cut to size on my chop saw. The tenons were marked and cut on a table saw using a self-built jig, courtesy of Bob Wearing's *Making Woodwork Aids and Devices*, *see panel*.

Because the saw's crown guard and riving knife have to be removed for this, ensure that adequate guarding is built into the jig. The shoulders were removed using a cut-off box on the table saw, again ensuring accurate repeat cuts.

Unless a random effect is desired, carefully mark the direction for the tenons' diagonal wedges on their ends.

The drawer runners require cutting to length and stub tenoning into the mortices cut into the bearer rails. I cut these tenons by clamping two runners at a time end-to-end in the vice, then routed them using a side fence and straight cutter.

The carcass requires a rebate cut to

accommodate the back panel. Again, this is best done with the router, side fence and straight cutter.

Carcass assembly

Cutting the tails on the uprights means gluing all the carcass components together at the same time. Preparation is everything, taking into account time, space, clamps and blocks, wedges all cut to size and a slow-setting glue such as Cascamite – plus, preferably, some assistance.

Attempting this task single-handed is rather foolish but even so this is my preferred way of working. Helpers can be the biggest liability and, where possible, I take

ABOVE:
Graduating the drawer sizes is a traditional device that adds a pleasing sense of proportion

RIGHT: Another cabinetmaking tradition – 'English' dovetails with fine pins
BELOW: Detail of drawer runner and rail construction

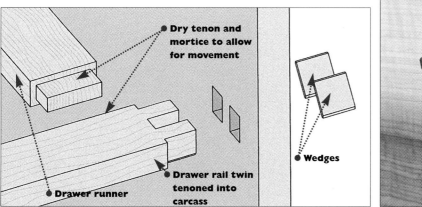

- Dry tenon and mortice to allow for movement
- Wedges
- Drawer runner
- Drawer rail twin tenoned into carcass

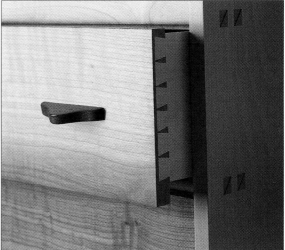

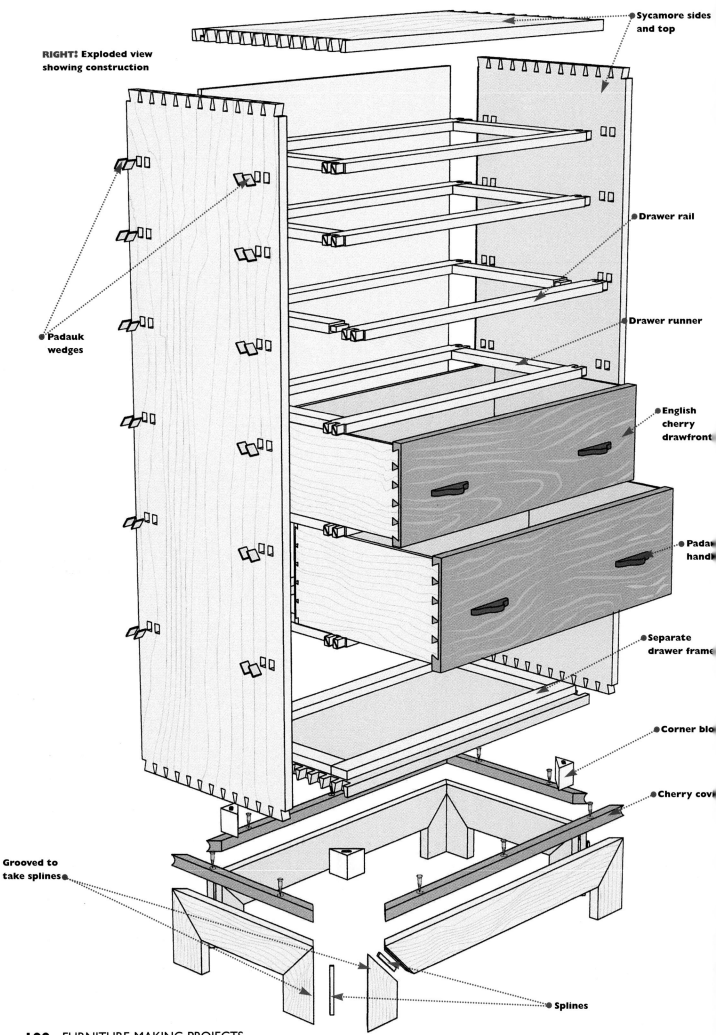

RIGHT: Exploded view
showing construction

Sycamore sides
and top

Drawer rail

Drawer runner

English
cherry
drawfront

Pada
handl

Separate
drawer frame

Corner blo

Cherry cov

Padauk
wedges

Grooved to
take splines

Splines

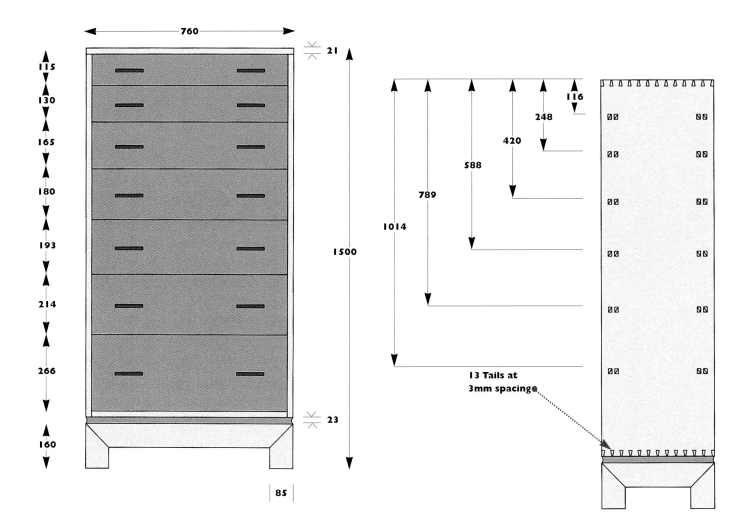

760

115
130
165
180
193
214
266
160

21

1500

23

85

116
248
420
588
789
1014

13 Tails at
3mm spacing

out my intemperance on any odd pieces of wood to hand or foot!

Glue is first applied to all surfaces to be joined, fitting the drawer runners into the bearer rails dry to allow for movement, then the bearer rails are fitted into their respective mortices in one carcass side, which are laid flat on blocks on the floor.

Next place the carcass top and bottom in position, fit one end of the second carcass side and gradually pivot the other end down, fitting the bearer rails one at a time; then, using a block and hammer, tap into place.

Raise the carcass into an upright position and apply clamps to bring the joints together – an awkward move as wedges must be placed into the tenons after they are pulled up but before they are obscured by clamping blocks.

Working from the top down, each section is clamped and wedges inserted; the clamps are then removed and placed upon the next section, the wedges proving adequate to hold the sides tight whilst drying.

The carcass is checked for square – and of course mine wasn't, though with the aid of a hefty pre-war 6ft T-bar cramp pulling across the diagonals, this was soon settled.

When dry, the protruding tenons were cut flush to the sides, cleaned up and sanded to 320 grit.

Drawers

The drawers are easy by comparison – only 150 dovetails 'hand-cut' on the bandsaw! The drawer gradings are determined by reference to the Hambridge Rectangles method, *see panel*.

The sycamore drawer-sides are thicknessed to 7mm, which looks right to me. The backs are 10mm white ash (*Fraxinus americana*). The fronts, back and sides require cross-cutting to size – I use a chop saw set perfectly square – finishing with a light touch across the grain with a bench plane.

Mark the dovetails; I prefer 'English' – very fine – dovetails for thinner sides. The tails are bandsawn and the waste chiselled out. The pins are then marked out onto the fronts from the sides using a sharp knife, sawn to the line and waste removed.

Drawer slips – with central muntins to spread the load – are used. The drawer bottoms are of cedar of Lebanon (*Cedrus libani*), which allows a lovely aroma to waft when opened.

Plinth

The mitred plinth was constructed from sycamore. Each leg is made up

HAMBRIDGE RECTANGLES

The Hambridge Rectangle proportioning system is based upon the Golden Section – the ratio 1.6180339 – developed by the Ancient Greeks, as adapted for modern usage by American mathematician Jay Hambridge.

The method requires a square, drawn to scale of the width of the proposed project. Extend the verticals of this square and, taking a compass and using the bottom right corner of the square as the datum, scribe an arc across the top left corner of the square to bisect the extended vertical.

From this intersection extend a horizontal line to form a rectangle; this is the first graduation, the square acting only as a guide. Continuing to extend arcs upwards creates a graduated scale which can be measured off and transferred to the project; due to the visual indication given, this works better, I feel, than a numbers-only method.

It also allows a height to be determined dependent upon the width chosen, though in my case the height was selected by circumstances and the gradings adapted slightly to fit.

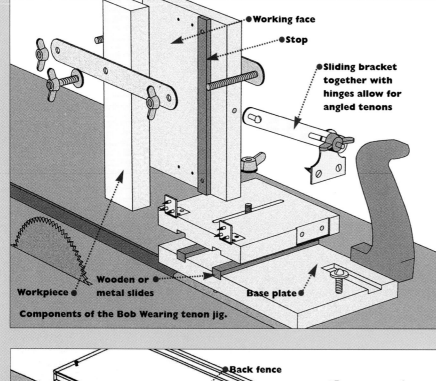

Working face

Stop

Sliding bracket together with hinges allow for angled tenons

Workpiece

Wooden or metal slides

Base plate

Components of the Bob Wearing tenon jig.

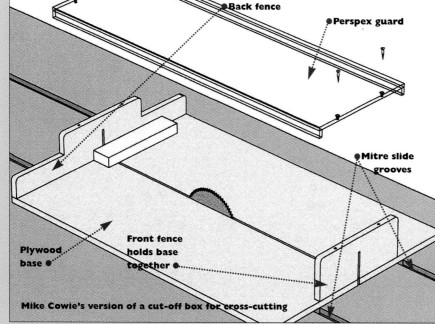

Back fence

Perspex guard

Mitre slide grooves

Plywood base

Front fence holds base together

Mike Cowie's version of a cut-off box for cross-cutting

Bob Wearing, in his book *Making Woodwork Aids & Devices*, has an excellent jig for cutting the cheeks of tenons. It uses the mitre-guide slots on a table saw, and is quite sophisticated in that it allows angled tenons to be cut. A simpler version could be made for 90° only operation.

The jig is constructed of birch ply with metal or wooden slides, with a clamp that can be made of either material. A slide allows the jig to be adjusted for different cuts and thicker tenons, and the stop can be made adjustable by drilling more than one set of holes in the vertical working face.

Once made the jig can be tested for accuracy by gauging a wide piece of scrap wood, then running it in the jig, adjusting until it is cut parallel with the gauged line.

As the table saw's riving knife and crown guard have to taken off for this jig, a separate guard will have to be made. A simple version is shown in Bob's book.

A cross-cutting box can also be made using the bed slots of a table saw. This is also made from plywood, the size depends on your saw. Start with the runners; these should be made to fit slightly below the level of the table, so that when they are screwed to the base they will ride free of the bottom of the groove. Once cut to size, put the base board against the rip fence – this will make sure it is square to the bed slots – then with the runners in their slots mark out and drill the screw holes. Screw and glue the runners in place, then make the front and rear fences. Attach the front fence only and make your first cut; not all the way through though! Once it is cutting true you can fix the rear main fence.

Making Woodwork Aids & Devices, by Robert Wearing, is available in paperback (revised edition, GMC Publications, 1999), ISBN 1 86108 129 4

from the same stock as the carcass material, and mitred to form an L-section. The rails are then mitred into the legs.

These were all jointed using grooves and splines. To give balance, cut and cove a strip of cherry, and fit it between the plinth and carcass to break up the sycamore.

The carcass is attached to the plinth with glued and screwed blocks across the inside corners – slot the holes to allow for movement.

Finishing

The drawer fronts are finished with Danish oil, rubbing down with 240 grit abrasive between applications over a period of a week with daily coatings.

The rest of the piece is finished with sanding sealer and white polish.

Handles are the bane of my life, possibly because I ignore them at the outset, preferring to leave them until last. However in this case, comments raised when the chest was awaiting them were to the effect that any

handles would spoil the front elevation. I was inclined to agree.

Expediency intervened, handle-less drawers only being opened with great difficulty. After playing with some scrap wood, I decided on a simple pull that could be cut with a router.

A jig was constructed and the required number cut from some spare padauk (*Pterocarpus soyauxii*). After applying a coat of sanding sealer to retard the darkening tendency of padauk, I rubbed down the handles and attached them with screws. ■

Budget brief

Guy Lewis makes a tall two-drawer cabinet in American cherry

PHOTOGRAPHY BY JOHN MORLEY

THE FEAR of disruption to work schedules, coupled with worry that clients may be put off by apparent chaos, results in many furniture-makers discouraging visits to workshops.

Personally I encourage such calls, having found a number of good clients this way; indeed, the piece of furniture featured here resulted from just such an encounter.

The brief was for a tall cabinet with two drawers and a cupboard base, with adjustable shelves, to measure 1353mm (53¼in) tall, 762mm (30in) wide and 381mm (15in) deep. The piece had to fit into a specific niche in the client's London home.

He favoured American cherry (*Prunus serotina*) for the cabinet, with handles of American black walnut (*Juglans niger*). We were working to a set budget, but this was eased by his willingness to let me work on it as and when other jobs allowed.

One constraint imposed by the budget was that a complicated or curvaceous piece would not be possible. I enjoy working within set parameters and the simple design I came up with, coupled with the choice of timber and dimensions, lent this piece a distinct Shaker air while remaining contemporary and original.

Carcass

The carcass comprises two cherry sides joined by four horizontal boards of the same thickness; these form the apertures for the drawers and bottom fixed shelf. For the sake of stability and economy I made these components from 18mm (¾in) two-sided cherry-faced plywood, with a solid cherry lipping.

As yet I have not been able to find a supplier of decorative plywood with two 'show' veneer faces, so I made these boards up from one sheet of 12mm (½in) one-sided cherry plywood and another of 6mm (¼in), laminated together good faces out.

103

Door recesses

The doors are fitted flush with the drawer fronts so must be recessed into the carcass sides. Before cutting this recess I made the doors slightly oversize in width and height, but to a finished thickness of 13mm (½in). The recess can then be cut to match the door's thickness.

Mark out the recess then cut close to the marked line on a bandsaw. I trim up to the line by clamping a straight-edge exactly on the line, then using this to guide a bearing-guided panel-trimming cutter in my router.

The adjustable shelves are supported by short lengths of 6mm (¼in) diameter copper rod which locate in a series of holes accurately drilled at the required height and matching both sides.

Any inaccuracy here will be very apparent when the shelves are fitted, and is virtually impossible to remedy with the carcass glued up. A real case of 'think three times, measure twice and drill once'!

When using this means of adjusting the shelves, I have found that sanding the copper rod with 120 grit abrasive to slightly less than 6mm (¼in) eases removal and replacement.

Once the shelf-support holes have been drilled, the rebate for the carcass back can now be cut. Here I use a bearing-guided rebate cutter, set to the depth of the housings.

Cut-out, boards

The curved cut-out at the bottom of the carcass sides is marked out using a piece of string and a pencil as a compass. I measured 75mm (3in) up from the bottom centre line, then made trial and error adjustments to the string

● **GUY LEWIS** is a professional cabinetmaker working in Sturminster Newton in Dorset. He can be contacted on 01258 471642.

> "Any inaccuracy will be virtually impossible to remedy with the carcass glued up. A real case of think three times, measure twice and drill once!"

The drawer divisions use stopped housings while the top is rebated and fixed with screws.

The sides are made up and cut to 1321 by 381mm (52 by 15in), and the stopped housings and rebate are marked up and routed out. Two straight-edges clamped one either side of the router base ensure that the router doesn't wander off line while making these cuts.

Taking several passes with the router for each joint achieves smoother results. The rounded ends to the housings, left by the router cutter, are squared up with a cornering chisel.

EASIER DRAWER RUNNING

Everybody has his own preferred method of making drawers, but I would like to mention a couple of things that I do in certain circumstances to ease the process.

When making the drawer fronts, and if I have good access from the back, I mark in pencil the exact size and shape of the aperture onto the back of the oversized drawer front, then use a straight-edge-guided router to trim to the pencil line; this ensures a good fit even if the aperture is not absolutely square. To reduce breakout trim the end-grain first, then the long-grain.

To make sure that the drawers run easily I sometimes guide the drawer sides by pinning and gluing battens to the carcass; these are easily fitted from the back.

With the drawer fully in its aperture, they are attached to run against the inner drawer sides just below the drawer bottom and provide support for a potentially over-loaded drawer; they also act as drawer stops.

Glued and pinned battens provide guides for drawers

MAIN ILLUSTRATION BY IAN HALL

To make the handles, a block of walnut approximately 150 by 150 by 32mm (6 by 6 by 1¼in) is shaped to the profile of the handles, *see diagram*. The recess for the finger pull is cut using a bearing-guided rebate bit mounted in a router table; take care to enter and exit the handle without removing any material from the ends, *see diagram*.

Moving to the saw bench, slice off a suitable thickness for a finished 20mm (⅞in) handle, repeating the process until enough handles are made. I have found American black walnut to be fairly brittle when routed, so I always make up one or two spares just in case anything goes wrong.

Making the handles this way ensures that each one is identical and also that one's fingers are kept away from the cutter. Finally, the square edges are profiled with a small diameter round-over bit, using a simple holding device for safety.

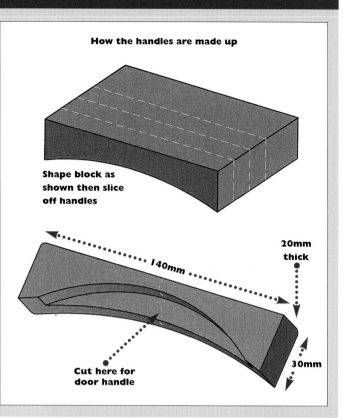

How the handles are made up

Shape block as shown then slice off handles

140mm

20mm thick

30mm

Cut here for door handle

Handle detail showing rebate

until the correct curve was achieved.

I then cut close to the line using a jigsaw then, using a circular plane followed by abrasive paper, smoothed the curve.

Having formed the curve on one side it can be used as a template for the other. As with the door recesses, a router is fitted with a bearing-guided cutter which follows the first side to cut the second.

A solid cherry lipping is biscuit-jointed to the four horizontal carcass members using No. 0 size biscuits. Once this is done they can be cut to size and trimmed for a good fit in the housed sides. Obviously the bottom fixed board will need to be 13mm (½in) shallower than the others to accommodate the doors.

Before gluing up I always do a dry run to ensure that everything is close to hand, that the sash cramps are at the correct length, and that it will all go together square.

With the carcass glued up it's time to make and fit the drawers, *see panel*.

Hinges are fitted to the carcass and then to the doors; when satisfied with the fit, remove the doors and mark up the curved

cut-out using the pencil and string method outlined above. Using the method of templating one side from the other guarantees a symmetrical result.

Raising the bottom of the doors slightly allows for the thickness of a carpet. Each door is kept shut with two spring-loaded ball-bearing cabinet catches.

Handles, shelves

The cabinet is then assembled and the positions for the handles, *see panel*, marked. These are attached to the drawers with two screws each – the cupboard handles are slightly trickier, being a single handle cut in half;

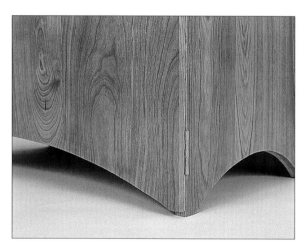

ABOVE: Curves set out with string and a pencil

TOP LEFT: Drawer detail

BOTTOM LEFT: Copper rod used as adjustable shelf supports – holes must be precisely drilled

"I carefully painted the rear of the cabinet with matt black paint to cover the ugly non-show side of the plywood"

this provides less area to take the screws and therefore requires absolute accuracy when drilling.

Also fitted at this stage are the cupboard's two 13mm (½in) solid cherry height-adjustable shelves, one full depth, the other half depth.

The solid top has a finished thickness of 32mm (1¼in) and overhangs the sides and front by 20mm (¹³⁄₁₆in). Before fixing, the square edges of the upper and lower faces are profiled with a ½in bearing-guided round-over router bit.

It is jointed to the top horizontal carcass member with No. 20 biscuits and four No. 8 screws. For economy, the back is made of 10mm one-sided cherry plywood with the good face inside the cabinet.

I carefully painted the rear of the cabinet with matt black paint to cover the ugly, non-show side of the plywood back.

Finish

When happy with the assembled cabinet, take it apart and sand to 320 grit. A coat of linseed oil thinned slightly with white spirit to aid absorption is applied inside and out.

When the oil is dry, give the whole piece a thin brush coat of shellac sanding sealer. When this is dry, wax along the grain with 0000 wire wool, following this with three more coats of wax. Many woods benefit from this form of finish and, although quite slow and laborious, it is my personal favourite.

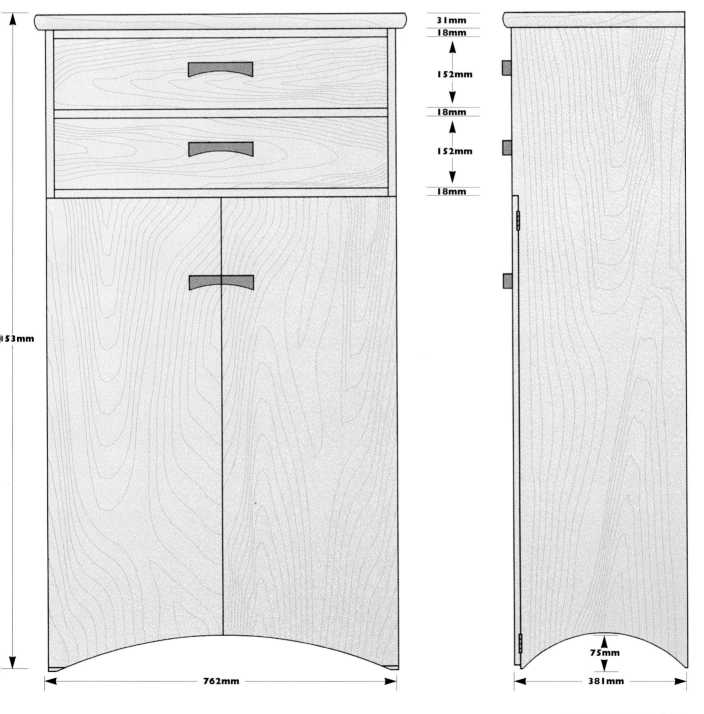

Second edition

PHOTOGRAPHY BY STEPHEN HEPWORTH   MAIN ILLUSTRATIONS BY IAN HALL

Andrew Lawton makes a chevron desk and chair

● **ANDREW LAWTON, a member of the Society of Designer Craftsmen, has been making furniture full time since 1980. He rescued Goatscliffe Workshops – run by pioneer craftsman Ben Coopland from the 1920s to the 1960s in Grindleford, Derbyshire – from near dereliction. Lawton's 1991 Spiral Table in English walnut inlaid with sycamore received a Guild Mark from the Worshipful Company of Furniture Makers.**

THIS DESK AND CHAIR are almost identical repeats of pieces which I produced in 1992-3 as speculative exhibition pieces. The originals were in ripple sycamore (*Acer pseudoplatanus*); the sequels in wych elm (*Ulmas glabra*).

The design came about after much sketching and doodling, in an attempt to create pieces that were both practical and attractive. I am an admirer of Art Deco furniture and architecture but, temperamentally, I feel most at home with the restrained wholesomeness of Arts and Crafts work. These influences, coupled with the known rigid properties inherent in corrugated structures, put me on the road.

Essentially, any writing surface which quivers or vibrates in use, no matter how beautiful, is a failure as a design – although, if that turned out to be the case, you could always re-launch it as a hall table and side-step the problem!

What finally clinched the design was the acquisition of some spectacular solid ripple sycamore which somehow had slipped through the net and escaped being sliced into veneers. I hoped that the ripple of the grain, at right angles to the shaping of the desk sides, would look good.

Second desk

The second desk and chair were commissioned by a client who already had a small table of mine in wych elm, and wanted the new pieces to match. Other designer craftsmen have said that they don't like repeating a design because subsequent versions lack the creative excitement of the first – repeats becoming lifeless copies of the original. There is much truth in this. You can become totally wrapped up in a new piece, and get a real buzz if it all comes off – whereas a repeated design can sometimes feel a bit of an anti-climax. On the other hand, from a practical standpoint, repeats offer the near certainty, although you can never be entirely sure with wood, that all the constructional headaches have been sorted out, and, vital for the professional maker, the job will be profitable.

The desk

After a good period of secondary seasoning all the components for the desk are machined to size, allowing for a final hand-planing. The ends are made first, using a tilt arbor table saw to form the angled joints, followed by assembly of the top. Ply tongues are inserted between the edges to add strength, and help line everything up. Regular readers will know that I prefer loose tongues to biscuits, but now that at least one firm makes beech ply biscuits, I have overcome my prejudice and will be getting a biscuit jointer myself before long!

RIGHT: Art Deco styling influenced the design of this desk and chair

FAR LEFT:
Assembled chair
back showing
mortice and
housing for
laminated arm

LEFT: Spreading
Cascamite on the
pre-bent
laminates

"We considered the resulting arms to be highly successful and immensely strong"

Variation on a theme

Once they had been cleaned up, the ends and top are marked out for the front and back drawer rail mortices, the four sets of double tenons, and the housings in the apexes of the inner faces which accommodate the drawer runners. The rails are similarly marked out. All this is done with a sharp marking knife and gauges for accuracy. The parallelogram-shaped mortice and tenons are a variation of a classic Arts and Crafts jointing method. I wouldn't have the temerity to claim that I'm the first to have done them like this, but I've never seen any made quite in this way. They are a little more difficult to cut than the usual through tenon and require some patient work with razor sharp chisels to make a neat job.

Once this stage is reached the top is offered up to the ends, and the chevron-shaped housings marked directly from one to the other. These are then routed out and cleaned up with a chisel.

The drawer rails, runners, and dust panels are straightforward, with due allowance made for movement across the grain. I am always banging on about this, but it is surprising how even professional makers sometimes fail to take this into account when designing in solid timber. The drawer divisions are stub tenoned into the rails and top. I felt that taking them through would be overdoing it, and might detract from the overall appearance of the desk.

Gluing-up

The whole drawer runner and rail assembly and ends are glued-up with the aid of softwood blocks temporarily glued on, and left to set after numerous checks to ensure all is square and true.

Next, the three back panels are made, and all internal surfaces which can't be reached once the top is in place are waxed and buffed up. The top is glued on and the black walnut wedges driven home – but not before you've made sure that the back panels are in their grooves. Having once glued-up a carcass and forgotten to insert the panels I always do a double check! Many makers glue-up at the end of the working day so that the glue can cure overnight and the piece be ready to work on in the morning; but there is a lot to be said for carrying out this rather vital operation earlier in the day when you are more fresh and alert!

Drawers

The drawers are made in the conventional way, dovetailed back and front, with oak (*Quercus spp*) sides and backs, and cedar of Lebanon (*Cedrus libani*) bottoms. Shaped pulls of walnut (*Juglans regia*) are fixed to the drawer fronts with stub mortice and tenons.

The chair

The design of the accompanying chair obviously had to match that of the desk, or at least be stylistically similar. I aimed to do this by giving the chair back the same chevron shaping as the desk ends. The inner face of the back gently curves to provide a comfortable support for the occupant's spine. As a contrast to the crisp angles of the desk, the arms are shaped to spring from the back to the front legs in sweeping arcs.

Each arm is built up from 2.5mm (³⁄₃₂ in) thick laminates, cut on the bandsaw, assembled in a jig consisting of male and female formers with cut-outs to accept G clamps. Made of MDF, the jig was devised with the help of Mark Applegate who was sharing my workshop at the time, and drew on the expertise he had gained during his course at Hooke Park. Partly to reduce the stress on the glue lines, but as much as anything to ease assembly, the laminates are pre-steam bent to roughly the final curvature. We considered the resulting arms to be highly successful and immensely strong.

BELOW: Tenon and housing joint from arm into the back of the chair

"What finally clinched it was the acquisition of some spectacular solid ripple sycamore which somehow had slipped through the net and escaped being sliced into veneers"

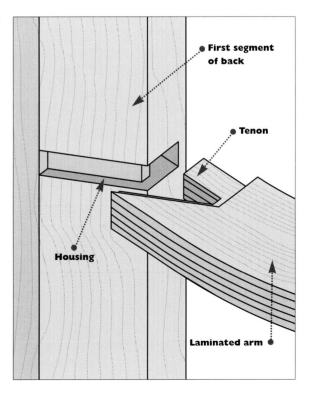

First segment of back

Tenon

Housing

Laminated arm

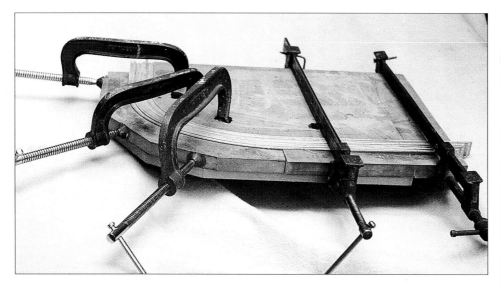

ABOVE: Arm gluing-up in jig

> "Having once glued-up a carcass and forgotten to insert the panels I always do a double check!"

Learning from the past

When I started out, I took on repair work as well as making new, out of economic necessity and a naive belief that the people whose old furniture I patched up would also commission me to make new pieces, which rarely happened. I didn't enjoy this work since I had neither been trained in restoration techniques nor have the temperament for it, but at least I learned first hand how and why old furniture fails, and try to minimise future problems in my own work. Thus the arms of these two desk chairs are joined to their backs with a substantial tenon and housed in at the same time, *see photographs*, with the aim that any outward pressure from the sitter's arms actually tightens the joint rather than forcing it apart, in a similar way to opening a drawer which, in theory at least, tightens the dovetails.

Continuing the theme of sound construction, the front legs are dovetailed to the arms, orientated so that they won't pull apart with repeated lifting of the chair by its arms.

The front seat rail is single tenoned to the legs. In turn, two rails which support the seat are doubled tenoned and wedged into it – these are then through tenoned into the back.

The seat itself is simply a shaped ply base, beautifully upholstered by Michael Davies of my nearby Derbyshire village of Foolow.

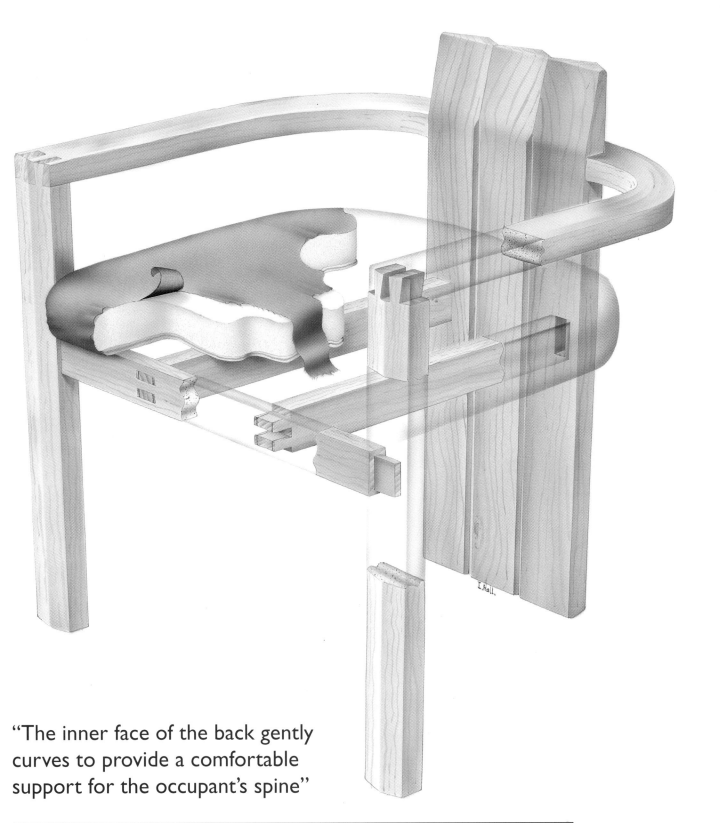

"The inner face of the back gently curves to provide a comfortable support for the occupant's spine"

TIMBER SELECTION

The timber for these pieces came from a huge tree which I bought as a freshly felled log in the mid-80's – a victim of Dutch elm disease – and had sawn into various thicknesses at a local mill. It has been in stick since then, out in the open air covered with old sheets of corrugated iron to keep the rain and sun off. Never put iron or steel sheets over oak, by the way, or the timber may end up stained blue-black, as when an old nail is embedded in it.

After all this time the elm is as well air dried as it ever will be. The main drawback to seasoning and storing timber in this way is that it is prone to infestation by the furniture beetle. This generally seems to attack only the sapwood of elm, or boards which are a bit dodgy, that I would avoid using anyway. Suspect planks must be carefully checked and, if they have to go, can at least be cut up into firewood.

The various parts of the chair and desk were roughed out and stacked in the warmest part of the workshop, allowing air to circulate freely, and left for a couple of months until the moisture content had fallen to 10 or 11 %. The success of a piece of furniture relies heavily on careful timber selection. For example, make sure that a row of drawer fronts are all cut from the same board. If it is not possible to get a good grain match between adjacent boards, then adapt the design to make a deliberate feature of this.

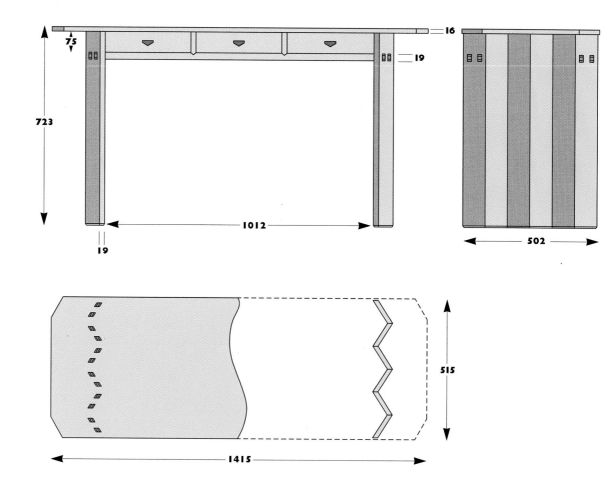

Finishing

The original ripple sycamore desk and chair were sanded down to 400 grit and sprayed with pre-catalysed lacquer, which is my preferred finish on most light coloured woods which don't have to work hard for a living. If hard wear is likely then an acid catalyst lacquer would be used.

The almost unreal figure of the timber, combined with the finish, led several people to remark that it was hard to believe it was actually wood – I'm not sure if that is a compliment or not! Such a finish is in my view not appropriate to an open grained timber like elm, so the sequels are sanded to 280 grit and given several coats of Danish oil, carefully steel wooled and cleaned off between coats, then buffed up with a soft cloth.

Having recently seen the sycamore pieces again – the couple who bought them have gone on to commission several more items – I'm still not sure whether I prefer the design in one timber or the other, but it reminded me what an amazingly versatile material we have available to us, as woodworkers. ■

BELOW LEFT:
Arm joint showing 'ear' to assist assembly

BELOW RIGHT:
Arm to leg dovetails offered up

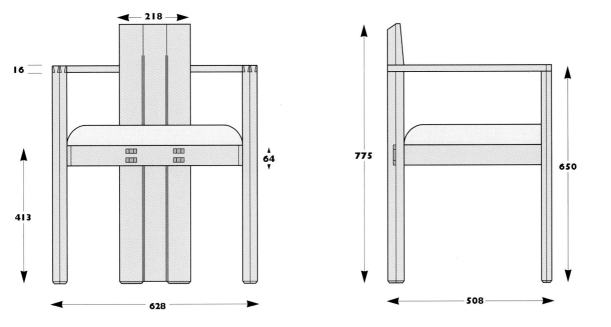

218

16

413

64

628

775

508

47

47   32

"Repeats offer the near certainty that all the constructional headaches have been sorted out, and the job will be profitable"

**RIGHT: Desk and chair –
note sweep of arms into
back and wedged tenon
from seat support rails**

Shelving some p

Peter Scaife takes a piece of lime straight from the bandsaw to make a set of book shelves

● **PETER SCAIFE** trained as a woodwork teacher during the late 1950s and early 1960s at the former Borough Road and Trent Park Colleges, but found that while he loved woodwork he hated teaching, so switched to woodworking journalism. He describes his experience as broad rather than deep, ranging from boat-building to sculpture.

BELOW LEFT: The dilemma and the challenge – lime ripped by the local sawmill produced tapered boards

BELOW MIDDLE: Simple but effective – a feature is made of the fixings

THIRTY YEARS AGO, in the first warm glow of marriage, I told my new wife I'd make her a hall table. It'll be an elegant long-legged piece, I said, with a half-round top probably made from satinwood enhanced with marquetry and fine stringing.

Well, I didn't actually promise…

…So – how about some shelving, I asked her? She agreed.

I had in my workshop a 1000mm (39½in) by 400mm (15¾in) by 75mm (3in) piece of lime (*Tilia vulgaris*) left over from a carving of Christ that I had done for a Norfolk church 20 years ago.

My muscles having become softer and the timber harder, conversion by hand was out of the question, so I asked the timber yard to tidy up the edges, rip it down the centre and deep-saw it into eight boards of about 1000mm (39½in) by 180mm (7in) by 18mm (¾in).

Instead of putting it through a circular saw to produce all eight pieces of the same dimension, a power-fed bandsaw which did not cut in a straight line resulted in timber ranging in thickness from 12mm (½in) to 37mm (1⁷⁄₁₆in), some of it curved along its length but none in wind.

Design opportunity

In this kind of situation you remember that there is no rule book.

No law exists that says every member of a piece of furniture has to be of equal thickness, has to be flat and has to be planed smooth. Design nannies do not exist.

Lime, being devoid of figure, of even colour and very crisp, is ideal for carving. The band-sawing had given it a pleasing texture; sunlight raking across it revealed small, regular ridges across the grain. My mind was made up – use it as it is, in the knowledge that any marks on the precious surface cannot be erased.

Because the texture could never be replicated, the first job, before marking out even, is to put on a coat of hard, clear varnish.

Only after that can the next stage in the mental design process be pondered: with the best two, slightly curved, pieces chosen for the sides, would they slope in or out? I set the lower ends vertical to the floor, sloping them slightly outwards at the top.

The four shelves start with the thickest at the bottom, with the thinnest at the top and the slight concavities upwards.

Fixing to sides

My next conundrum was how to join the shelves to the sides.

Because the sides are not parallel, the housing is tricky to mark out. I discarded the possibility of using through tenons because of the problem posed by their ends: smooth and flush would result in a clash of texture; allowing them to stand slightly proud would be too arty-crafty; but something brass would look good.

Countersunk screws are too ordinary, and cannot be screwed into end-grain. Look for bolts in the ironmongers, and find brass, 6mm by 40mm, pan-head, parallel-sided screws to be fixed into holes drilled in the ends of the shelves.

Instead of using glue – too risky – or chemical filler – unknown quantity – consider fixing nuts into the underside of the shelf, about 20mm (¾in) from the end.

This means a little 10mm by 3mm mortice must be cut to take a square, zinc-plated nut.

> "No law exists that says every member of a piece of furniture has to be of equal thickness, has to be flat and has to be planed smooth. Design nannies do not exist"

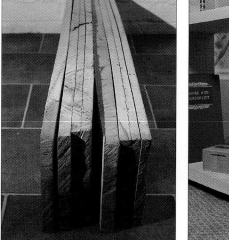

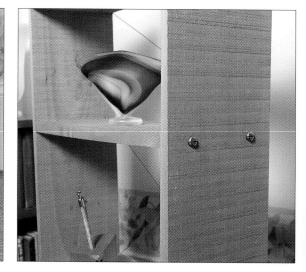

oblems

"Picture wire zig-zagging across the back and stapled in position adds greatly to the overall effect"

Back to the rule book: who says mortices must be rectangular? Why not round? A trial run in scrap timber demonstrates that a hole drilled to 10mm (⅜in) allows the nut to wobble, so make it 8mm (⅝₆in) with a Forstner bit to achieve a flat bottom, chopping out just over 1mm on each side.

The result is remarkably stiff, but will it need some additional rigidity – perhaps some triangulation at the back with brass picture wire? *see right.*

Drill all the holes for the two lower shelves; where the sides are parallel, chisel out grooves for the nuts, put them in, offer up the screws and tighten them. Offer up the next two shelves, mark the length required and drill more holes.

In fact, these 16 nuts and screws, with copper washers under their heads for the sake of appearance, do make for a rigid structure, but picture wire zig-zagging across the back and stapled in position adds greatly to the overall effect.

Cleaning up

All that remains is to clean up the front edges with a smoothing plane. I applied a blue-grey stain to the back edges, but found this added nothing, so varnished the front edges to match the rest.

So what did I gain from this? While many traditions are to be respected – and I'm very glad I once made a cabinet with secret lapped dovetails, all hand-cut, and then French polished it – taking a risk by innovating and experimenting is fun.

When success comes, it is all the more welcome – especially when the result has relied not on drawing but on eye and imagination alone. ■

LEFT: Bottom shelf detail – note the smooth planed finish to the whole of the front edge, in contrast to the sawn sides and shelves

RIGHT: A design that evolved from the material

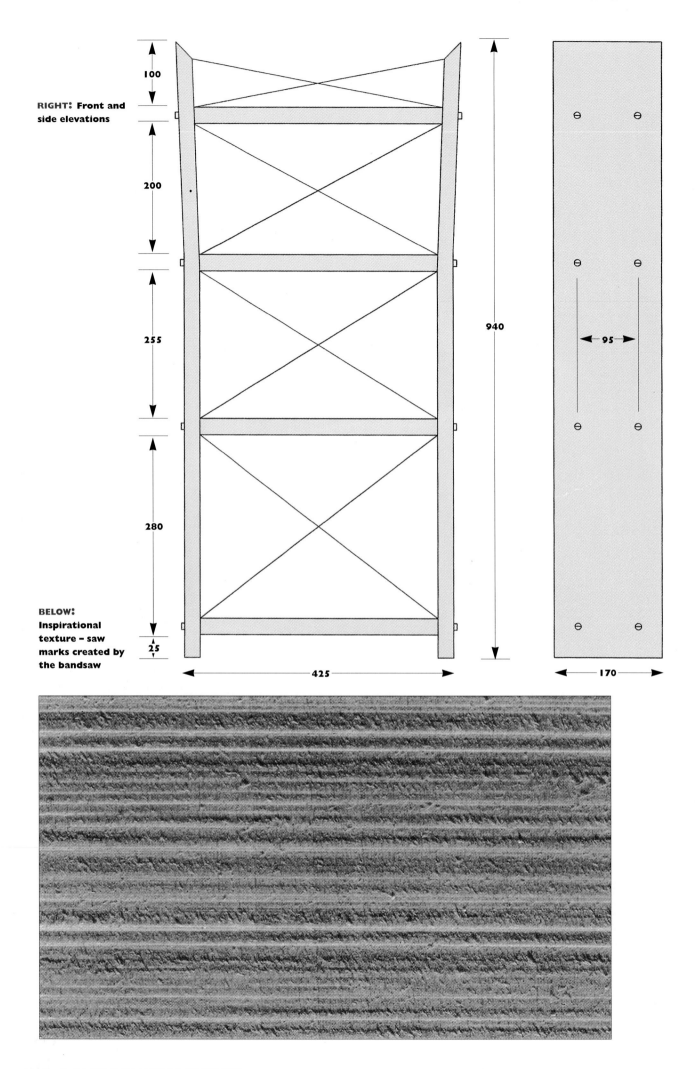

100

RIGHT: Front and side elevations

200

255

940

95

280

BELOW: Inspirational texture – saw marks created by the bandsaw

25

425

170

METRIC/IMPERIAL CONVERSION CHART

mm	inch	mm	inch	mm	inch	mm	inch	
1	0.03937	26	1.02362	60	2.36220	310	12.20472	1 mm = 0.03937 inch
2	0.07874	27	1.06299	70	2.75590	320	12.59842	1 cm = 0.3937 inch
3	0.11811	28	1.10236	80	3.14960	330	12.99212	1 m = 3.281 feet
4	0.15748	29	1.14173	90	3.54330	340	13.38582	1 inch = 25.4 mm
5	0.19685	30	1.18110	100	3.93700	350	13.77952	1 foot = 304.8 mm
								1 yard = 914.4 mm
6	0.23622	31	1.22047	110	4.33070	360	14.17322	
7	0.27559	32	1.25984	120	4.72440	370	14.56692	
8	0.31496	33	1.29921	130	5.11811	380	14.96063	
9	0.35433	34	1.33858	140	5.51181	390	15.35433	
10	0.39370	35	1.37795	150	5.90551	400	15.74803	
11	0.43307	36	1.41732	160	6.29921	410	16.14173	
12	0.47244	37	1.45669	170	6.69291	420	16.53543	
13	0.51181	38	1.49606	180	7.08661	430	16.92913	
14	0.55118	39	1.53543	190	7.48031	440	17.32283	
15	0.59055	40	1.57480	200	7.87401	450	17.71653	
16	0.62992	41	1.61417	210	8.26771	460	18.11023	
17	0.66929	42	1.65354	220	8.66141	470	18.50393	
18	0.70866	43	1.69291	230	9.05511	480	18.89763	
19	0.74803	44	1.73228	240	9.44881	490	19.29133	
20	0.78740	45	1.77165	250	9.84252	500	19.68504	
21	0.82677	46	1.81102	260	10.23622			
22	0.86614	47	1.85039	270	10.62992			
23	0.90551	48	1.88976	280	11.02362			
24	0.94488	49	1.92913	290	11.41732			
25	0.98425	50	1.96850	300	11.81102			

IMPERIAL/METRIC CONVERSION CHART

inch		mm	inch		mm	inch		mm
0	0	0	23/64	0.359375	9.1281	45/64	0.703125	17.8594
1/64	0.015625	0.3969				23/32	0.71875	18.2562
1/32	0.03125	0.7938	3/8	0.375	9.5250	47/64	0.734375	18.6531
3/64	0.046875	1.1906	25/64	0.390625	9.9219			
1/16	0.0625	1.5875	13/32	0.40625	10.3188	3/4	0.750	19.0500
			27/64	0.421875	10.7156			
5/64	0.078125	1.9844				49/64	0.765625	19.4469
3/32	0.09375	2.3812	7/16	0.4375	11.1125	25/32	0.78125	19.8438
7/64	0.109375	2.7781	29/64	0.453125	11.5094	51/64	0.796875	20.2406
			15/32	0.46875	11.9062	13/16	0.8125	20.6375
1/8	0.125	3.1750	31/64	0.484375	12.3031			
9/64	0.140625	3.5719				53/64	0.828125	21.0344
5/32	0.15625	3.9688	1/2	0.500	12.700	27/32	0.84375	21.4312
11/64	0.171875	4.3656	33/64	0.515625	13.0969	55/64	0.858375	21.8281
			17/32	0.53125	13.4938			
3/16	0.1875	4.7625	35/64	0.546875	13.8906	7/8	0.875	22.2250
13/64	0.203125	5.1594	9/16	0.5625	14.2875	57/64	0.890625	22.6219
7/32	0.21875	5.5562				29/32	0.90625	23.0188
15/64	0.234375	5.9531	37/64	0.578125	14.6844	59/64	0.921875	23.4156
1/4	0.250	6.3500	19/32	0.59375	15.0812			
			39/64	0.609375	15.4781	15/16	0.9375	23.8125
17/64	0.265625	6.7469				61/64	0.953125	24.2094
9/32	0.28125	7.1438	5/8	0.625	15.8750	31/32	0.96875	24.6062
19/64	0.296875	7.5406	41/64	0.640625	16.2719	63/64	0.984375	25.0031
5/16	0.3125	7.9375	21/32	0.65625	16.6688			
			43/64	0.671875	17.0656			
21/64	0.1328125	8.3344						
11/32	0.34375	8.7312	11/16	0.6875	17.4625	1 inch = 1.000 = 25.40 mm		

INDEX

TITLES AVAILABLE FROM
GMC Publications
BOOKS

WOODCARVING

The Art of the Woodcarver	GMC Publications
Carving Architectural Detail in Wood: The Classical Tradition	
	Frederick Wilbur
Carving Birds & Beasts	GMC Publications
Carving the Human Figure: Studies in Wood and Stone	Dick Onians
Carving Nature: Wildlife Studies in Wood	Frank Fox-Wilson
Carving Realistic Birds	David Tippey
Decorative Woodcarving	Jeremy Williams
Elements of Woodcarving	Chris Pye
Essential Woodcarving Techniques	Dick Onians
Further Useful Tips for Woodcarvers	GMC Publications
Lettercarving in Wood: A Practical Course	Chris Pye
Making & Using Working Drawings for Realistic Model Animals	
	Basil F. Fordham
Power Tools for Woodcarving	David Tippey
Practical Tips for Turners & Carvers	GMC Publications
Relief Carving in Wood: A Practical Introduction	Chris Pye
Understanding Woodcarving	GMC Publications
Understanding Woodcarving in the Round	GMC Publications
Useful Techniques for Woodcarvers	GMC Publications
Wildfowl Carving – Volume 1	Jim Pearce
Wildfowl Carving – Volume 2	Jim Pearce
Woodcarving: A Complete Course	Ron Butterfield
Woodcarving: A Foundation Course	Zoë Gertner
Woodcarving for Beginners	GMC Publications
Woodcarving Tools & Equipment Test Reports	GMC Publications
Woodcarving Tools, Materials & Equipment	Chris Pye

WOODTURNING

Adventures in Woodturning	David Springett
Bert Marsh: Woodturner	Bert Marsh
Bowl Turning Techniques Masterclass	Tony Boase
Colouring Techniques for Woodturners	Jan Sanders
Contemporary Turned Wood: New Perspectives in a Rich Tradition	
	Ray Leier, Jan Peters & Kevin Wallace
The Craftsman Woodturner	Peter Child
Decorative Techniques for Woodturners	Hilary Bowen
Fun at the Lathe	R.C. Bell
Illustrated Woodturning Techniques	John Hunnex
Intermediate Woodturning Projects	GMC Publications
Keith Rowley's Woodturning Projects	Keith Rowley
Practical Tips for Turners & Carvers	GMC Publications
Turning Green Wood	Michael O'Donnell
Turning Miniatures in Wood	John Sainsbury
Turning Pens and Pencils	Kip Christensen & Rex Burningham
Understanding Woodturning	Ann & Bob Phillips
Useful Techniques for Woodturners	GMC Publications
Useful Woodturning Projects	GMC Publications
Woodturning: Bowls, Platters, Hollow Forms, Vases, Vessels, Bottles, Flasks, Tankards, Plates	GMC Publications
Woodturning: A Foundation Course (New Edition)	Keith Rowley
Woodturning: A Fresh Approach	Robert Chapman
Woodturning: An Individual Approach	Dave Regester
Woodturning: A Source Book of Shapes	John Hunnex
Woodturning Jewellery	Hilary Bowen
Woodturning Masterclass	Tony Boase
Woodturning Techniques	GMC Publications
Woodturning Tools & Equipment Test Reports	GMC Publications
Woodturning Wizardry	David Springett

WOODWORKING

Advanced Scrollsaw Projects	GMC Publications
Bird Boxes and Feeders for the Garden	Dave Mackenzie
Complete Woodfinishing	Ian Hosker
David Charlesworth's Furniture-Making Techniques	
	David Charlesworth
The Encyclopedia of Joint Making	Terrie Noll
Furniture & Cabinetmaking Projects	GMC Publications
Furniture-Making Projects for the Wood Craftsman	GMC Publications
Furniture-Making Techniques for the Wood Craftsman	GMC Publications
Furniture Projects	Rod Wales
Furniture Restoration (Practical Crafts)	Kevin Jan Bonner
Furniture Restoration and Repair for Beginners	Kevin Jan Bonner
Furniture Restoration Workshop	Kevin Jan Bonner
Green Woodwork	Mike Abbott
Kevin Ley's Furniture Projects	Kevin Ley
Making & Modifying Woodworking Tools	Jim Kingshott
Making Chairs and Tables	GMC Publications
Making Classic English Furniture	Paul Richardson
Making Little Boxes from Wood	John Bennett
Making Screw Threads in Wood	Fred Holder
Making Shaker Furniture	Barry Jackson
Making Woodwork Aids and Devices	Robert Wearing
Mastering the Router	Ron Fox
Minidrill: Fifteen Projects	John Everett
Pine Furniture Projects for the Home	Dave Mackenzie
Practical Scrollsaw Patterns	John Everett
Router Magic: Jigs, Fixtures and Tricks to Unleash your Router's Full Potential	Bill Hylton
Routing for Beginners	Anthony Bailey
The Scrollsaw: Twenty Projects	John Everett
Sharpening: The Complete Guide	Jim Kingshott
Sharpening Pocket Reference Book	Jim Kingshott
Simple Scrollsaw Projects	GMC Publications
Space-Saving Furniture Projects	Dave Mackenzie
Stickmaking: A Complete Course	Andrew Jones & Clive George
Stickmaking Handbook	Andrew Jones & Clive George
Test Reports: The Router and Furniture & Cabinetmaking	
	GMC Publications
Veneering: A Complete Course	Ian Hosker
Veneering Handbook	Ian Hosker
Woodfinishing Handbook (Practical Crafts)	Ian Hosker
Woodworking with the Router: Professional Router Techniques any Woodworker can Use	
	Bill Hylton & Fred Matlack
The Workshop	Jim Kingshott

UPHOLSTERY

The Upholsterer's Pocket Reference Book	David James
Upholstery: A Complete Course (Revised Edition)	David James
Upholstery Restoration	David James
Upholstery Techniques & Projects	David James
Upholstery Tips and Hints	David James

TOYMAKING

Designing & Making Wooden Toys	*Terry Kelly*
Fun to Make Wooden Toys & Games	*Jeff & Jennie Loader*
Restoring Rocking Horses	*Clive Green & Anthony Dew*
Scrollsaw Toy Projects	*Ivor Carlyle*
Scrollsaw Toys for All Ages	*Ivor Carlyle*
Wooden Toy Projects	*GMC Publications*

DOLLS' HOUSES AND MINIATURES

1/12 Scale Character Figures for the Dolls' House	*James Carrington*
Architecture for Dolls' Houses	*Joyce Percival*
The Authentic Georgian Dolls' House	*Brian Long*
A Beginners' Guide to the Dolls' House Hobby	*Jean Nisbett*
Celtic, Medieval and Tudor Wall Hangings in 1/12 Scale Needlepoint	
	Sandra Whitehead
The Complete Dolls' House Book	*Jean Nisbett*
The Dolls' House 1/24 Scale: A Complete Introduction	*Jean Nisbett*
Dolls' House Accessories, Fixtures and Fittings	*Andrea Barham*
Dolls' House Bathrooms: Lots of Little Loos	*Patricia King*
Dolls' House Fireplaces and Stoves	*Patricia King*
Dolls' House Window Treatments	*Eve Harwood*
Easy to Make Dolls' House Accessories	*Andrea Barham*
Heraldic Miniature Knights	*Peter Greenhill*
How to Make Your Dolls' House Special: Fresh Ideas for Decorating	
	Beryl Armstrong
Make Your Own Dolls' House Furniture	*Maurice Harper*
Making Dolls' House Furniture	*Patricia King*
Making Georgian Dolls' Houses	*Derek Rowbottom*
Making Miniature Food and Market Stalls	*Angie Scarr*
Making Miniature Gardens	*Freida Gray*
Making Miniature Oriental Rugs & Carpets	*Meik & Ian McNaughton*
Making Period Dolls' House Accessories	*Andrea Barham*
Making Tudor Dolls' Houses	*Derek Rowbottom*
Making Victorian Dolls' House Furniture	*Patricia King*
Miniature Bobbin Lace	*Roz Snowden*
Miniature Embroidery for the Georgian Dolls' House	*Pamela Warner*
Miniature Embroidery for the Victorian Dolls' House	*Pamela Warner*
Miniature Needlepoint Carpets	*Janet Granger*
More Miniature Oriental Rugs & Carpets	*Meik & Ian McNaughton*
Needlepoint 1/12 Scale: Design Collections for the Dolls' House	
	Felicity Price
The Secrets of the Dolls' House Makers	*Jean Nisbett*

CRAFTS

American Patchwork Designs in Needlepoint	*Melanie Tacon*
A Beginners' Guide to Rubber Stamping	*Brenda Hunt*
Blackwork: A New Approach	*Brenda Day*
Celtic Cross Stitch Designs	*Carol Phillipson*
Celtic Knotwork Designs	*Sheila Sturrock*
Celtic Knotwork Handbook	*Sheila Sturrock*
Celtic Spirals and Other Designs	*Sheila Sturrock*
Collage from Seeds, Leaves and Flowers	*Joan Carver*
Complete Pyrography	*Stephen Poole*
Contemporary Smocking	*Dorothea Hall*
Creating Colour with Dylon	*Dylon International*
Creative Doughcraft	*Patricia Hughes*
Creative Embroidery Techniques Using Colour Through Gold	
	Daphne J. Ashby & Jackie Woolsey
The Creative Quilter: Techniques and Projects	*Pauline Brown*
Decorative Beaded Purses	*Enid Taylor*
Designing and Making Cards	*Glennis Gilruth*
Glass Engraving Pattern Book	*John Everett*
Glass Painting	*Emma Sedman*
Handcrafted Rugs	*Sandra Hardy*

How to Arrange Flowers: A Japanese Approach to English Design	
	Taeko Marvelly
How to Make First-Class Cards	*Debbie Brown*
An Introduction to Crewel Embroidery	*Mave Glenny*
Making and Using Working Drawings for Realistic Model Animals	
	Basil F. Fordham
Making Character Bears	*Valerie Tyler*
Making Decorative Screens	*Amanda Howes*
Making Fairies and Fantastical Creatures	*Julie Sharp*
Making Greetings Cards for Beginners	*Pat Sutherland*
Making Hand-Sewn Boxes: Techniques and Projects	*Jackie Woolsey*
Making Knitwear Fit	*Pat Ashforth & Steve Plummer*
Making Mini Cards, Gift Tags & Invitations	*Glennis Gilruth*
Making Soft-Bodied Dough Characters	*Patricia Hughes*
Natural Ideas for Christmas: Fantastic Decorations to Make	
	Josie Cameron-Ashcroft & Carol Cox
Needlepoint: A Foundation Course	*Sandra Hardy*
New Ideas for Crochet: Stylish Projects for the Home	*Darsha Capaldi*
Patchwork for Beginners	*Pauline Brown*
Pyrography Designs	*Norma Gregory*
Pyrography Handbook (Practical Crafts)	*Stephen Poole*
Ribbons and Roses	*Lee Lockheed*
Rose Windows for Quilters	*Angela Besley*
Rubber Stamping with Other Crafts	*Lynne Garner*
Sponge Painting	*Ann Rooney*
Stained Glass: Techniques and Projects	*Mary Shanahan*
Step-by-Step Pyrography Projects for the Solid Point Machine	
	Norma Gregory
Tassel Making for Beginners	*Enid Taylor*
Tatting Collage	*Lindsay Rogers*
Temari: A Traditional Japanese Embroidery Technique	*Margaret Ludlow*
Theatre Models in Paper and Card	*Robert Burgess*
Trip Around the World: 25 Patchwork, Quilting and Appliqué Projects	
	Gail Lawther
Trompe l'Oeil: Techniques and Projects	*Jan Lee Johnson*
Wool Embroidery and Design	*Lee Lockheed*

GARDENING

Auriculas for Everyone: How to Grow and Show Perfect Plants	
	Mary Robinson
Beginners' Guide to Herb Gardening	*Yvonne Cuthbertson*
Bird Boxes and Feeders for the Garden	*Dave Mackenzie*
The Birdwatcher's Garden	*Hazel & Pamela Johnson*
Broad-Leaved Evergreens	*Stephen G. Haw*
Companions to Clematis: Growing Clematis with Other Plants	
	Marigold Badcock
Creating Contrast with Dark Plants	*Freya Martin*
Creating Small Habitats for Wildlife in your Garden	*Josie Briggs*
Gardening with Wild Plants	*Julian Slatcher*
Growing Cacti and Other Succulents in the Conservatory and Indoors	
	Shirley-Anne Bell
Growing Cacti and Other Succulents in the Garden	*Shirley Anne Bell*
Hardy Perennials: A Beginner's Guide	*Eric Sawford*
The Living Tropical Greenhouse: Creating a Haven for Butterflies	
	John & Maureen Tampion
Orchids are Easy: A Beginner's Guide to their Care and Cultivation	
	Tom Gilland
Plant Alert: A Garden Guide for Parents	*Catherine Collins*
Planting Plans for Your Garden	*Jenny Shukman*
Plants that Span the Seasons	*Roger Wilson*
Sink and Container Gardening Using Dwarf Hardy Plants	
	Chris & Valerie Wheeler

PHOTOGRAPHY

An Essential Guide to Bird Photography	*Steve Young*
Light in the Landscape: A Photographer's Year	*Peter Watson*

VIDEOS

Drop-in and Pinstuffed Seats	*David James*	Twists and Advanced Turning	*Dennis White*
Stuffover Upholstery	*David James*	Sharpening the Professional Way	*Jim Kingshott*
Elliptical Turning	*David Springett*	Sharpening Turning & Carving Tools	*Jim Kingshott*
Woodturning Wizardry	*David Springett*	Bowl Turning	*John Jordan*
Turning Between Centres: The Basics	*Dennis White*	Hollow Turning	*John Jordan*
Turning Bowls	*Dennis White*	Woodturning: A Foundation Course	*Keith Rowley*
Boxes, Goblets and Screw Threads	*Dennis White*	Carving a Figure: The Female Form	*Ray Gonzalez*
Novelties and Projects	*Dennis White*	The Router: A Beginner's Guide	*Alan Goodsell*
Classic Profiles	*Dennis White*	The Scroll Saw: A Beginner's Guide	*John Burke*

MAGAZINES

WOODTURNING ◆ WOODCARVING ◆ FURNITURE & CABINETMAKING
THE ROUTER ◆ WOODWORKING ◆ THE DOLLS' HOUSE MAGAZINE
WATER GARDENING ◆ EXOTIC & GREENHOUSE GARDENING ◆ GARDEN CALENDAR
OUTDOOR PHOTOGRAPHY ◆ BLACK & WHITE PHOTOGRAPHY ◆ BusinessMatters

The above represents a full list of all titles currently published or scheduled to be published.
All are available direct from the Publishers or through bookshops, newsagents and specialist retailers.
To place an order, or to obtain a complete catalogue, contact:

**GMC Publications,
Castle Place, 166 High Street, Lewes, East Sussex BN7 1XU, United Kingdom
Tel: 01273 488005 Fax: 01273 478606
E-mail: pubs@thegmcgroup.com**

Orders by credit card are accepted